Novelty Songs

Piano Vocal Guitar

ISBN 0-88188-845-1

Hal Leonard Publishing Corporation

7777 West Bluemound Road   P.O. Box 13819   Milwaukee, Wisconsin 53213

The New Novelty Songbook

Piano Vocal Guitar

CONTENTS

ALLEY-OOP

Lively

By DALLAS FRAZIER

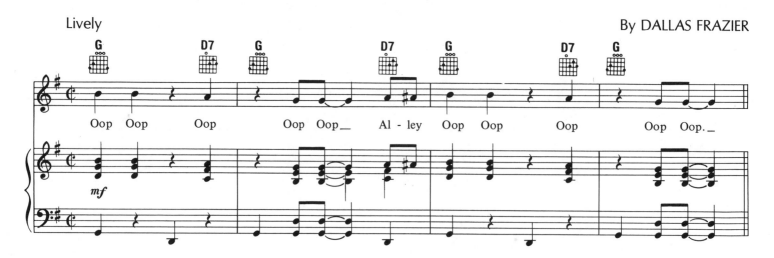

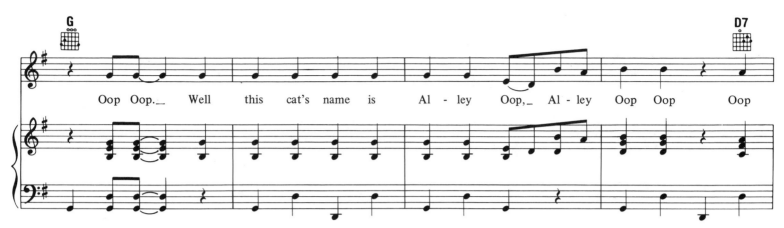

Oop Oop.__ Well this cat's name is Al - ley Oop,__ Al - ley Oop Oop Oop

Oop Oop.__ He's got a chauf - feur that's a gen - u - ine ___ di - no - saur,__ Al - ley
rides ___ through the jun - gle tear - in' limbs off of trees,__ Al - ley

Oop Oop Oop Oop Oop.__ And he can knuck - le your head__ be - fore you count to four, Al - ley
Oop Oop Oop Oop Oop.____ knock - in' great__ big mon - sters dead ___ on their knees, Al - ley

Oop Oop Oop Oop Oop.__ He's got a big ug - ly club and a head full of hair,__ Al - ley
Oop Oop Oop Oop Oop._____ The cats don't__ bug him 'cause they know__ bet - ter, Al - ley

Oop Oop Oop Oop Oop.___ Likes___ great big___ li-ons and___ griz-zly bears,___ Al-ley
Oop Oop Oop Oop Oop. 'Cause he's a mean mot-or scoot-er and a bad go get-ter, Al-ley

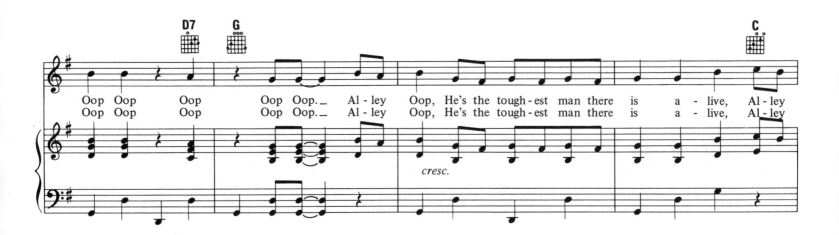

Oop Oop Oop Oop Oop.___ Al-ley Oop, He's the tough-est man there is a-live, Al-ley
Oop Oop Oop Oop Oop.___ Al-ley Oop, He's the tough-est man there is a-live, Al-ley

Oop, Wear-in' clothes from a wild cat's hide, Al-ley Oop, He's the king of the jun-gle jive___
Oop, Wear-in' clothes from a wild cat's hide, Al-ley Oop, He's the king of the jun-gle jive___

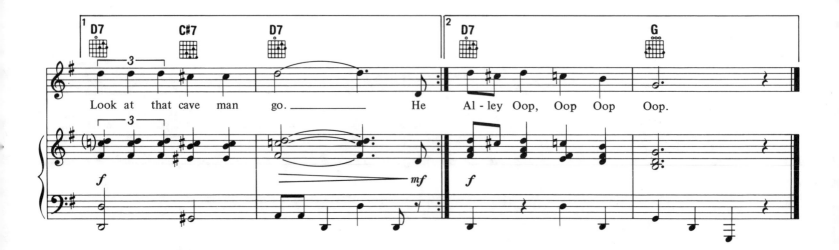

Look at that cave man go.___ He Al-ley Oop, Oop Oop Oop.

BABY SITTIN' BOOGIE

Moderate Boogie Tempo

Words and Music by
JOHNNY PARKER

(Coos, gurgles and any sort of baby sounds -) **My**
Girl version: When

girl _____ ba - by sits for some - one on her block, _____ then
I _____ ba - by sit for some - one on my block, _____ my

I come up and join her and we start to rock. _ The ba - by hears the beat and, man, it
guy comes up and joins me and we start to rock. _

is a shock _ when he goes *(Baby sounds - - - - - - - - -)* **A** { rock - in' type of boog - ie is the
know there is - n't an - y - one to

Optional - - - - - - - - - - -

taps his feet and sings (Baby sounds - - - - - - - - - - - - - - - -) he
group with the low down voice, (Baby sounds - - - - - - - - - - - - - - - -) and

is a hull - y gull - y bounc-ing ba - by boy, _ you know the rec - ord play - er is his
when it's time to tuck him in his lit - tle bed, _ with all that mu - sic run-ning through his

fav-'rite toy _ and don't for-get, he's ev - 'ry - bod - y's pride and joy _ when he goes
sleep - y head, _ the lit - tle fel - ler does-n't say good-night, in - stead _ he says,

(Baby sounds -) I (Goo goo goo goo boogie all - - - gone.)

BALLIN' THE JACK

Words by JIM BURRIS
Music by CHRIS SMITH

First you put your two knees close up tight, __ Then you sway 'em to the left, then you

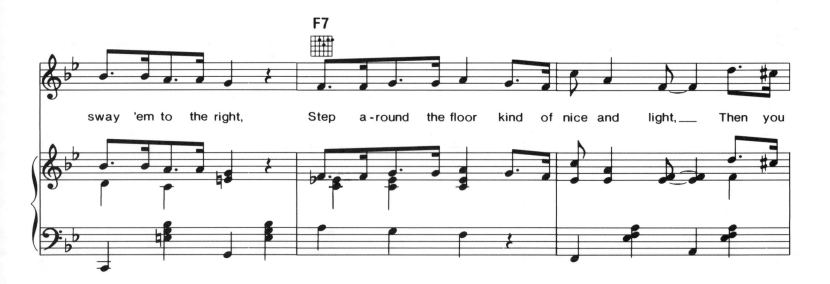

sway 'em to the right, Step a-round the floor kind of nice and light, __ Then you

THE BUNNY HOP

By RAY ANTHONY
and LEONARD AULETTI

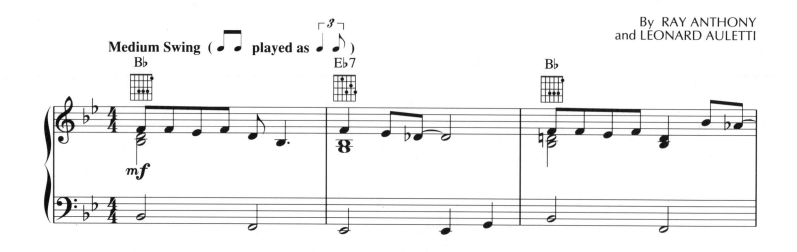

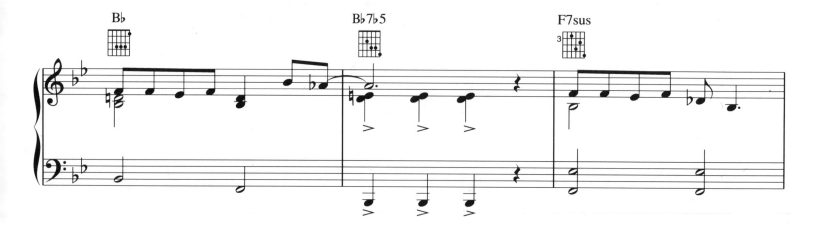

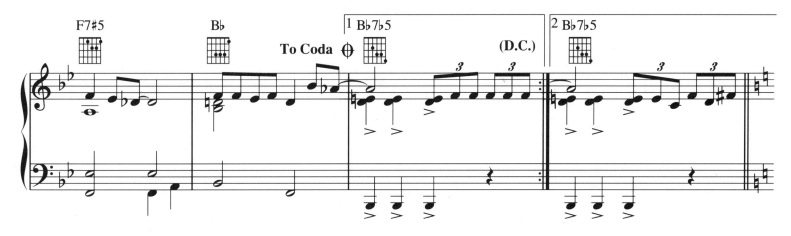

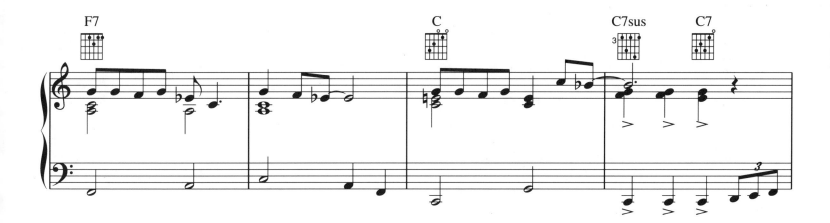

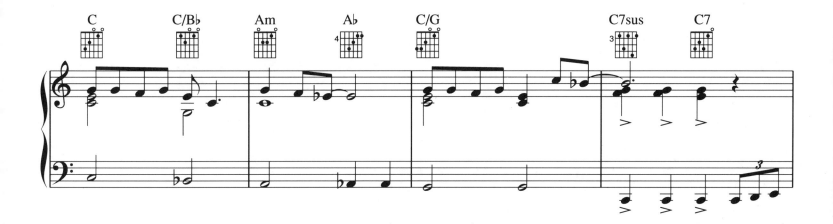

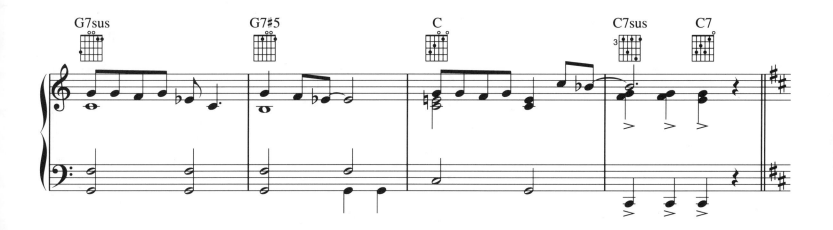

14

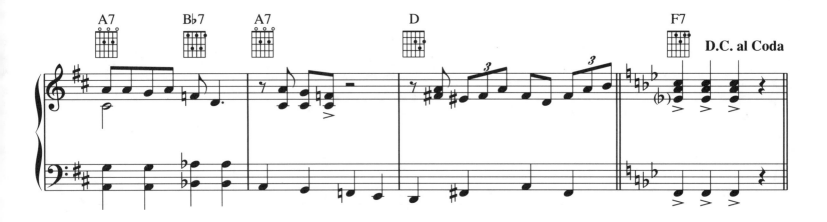

COLLEGIATE

By MOE JAFFE
and NAT BONX

Moderately

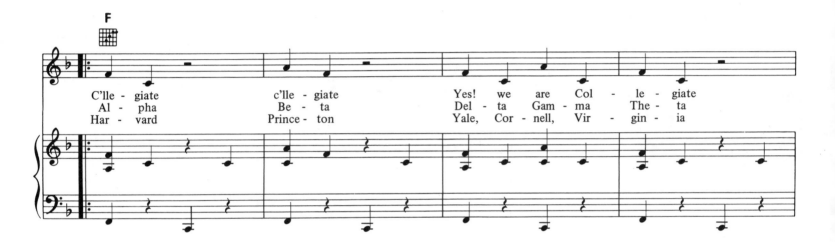

C'lle - giate   c'lle - giate   Yes! we are Col - le - giate
Al - pha   Be - ta   Del - ta Gam - ma The - ta
Har - vard   Prince - ton   Yale, Cor - nell, Vir - gin - ia

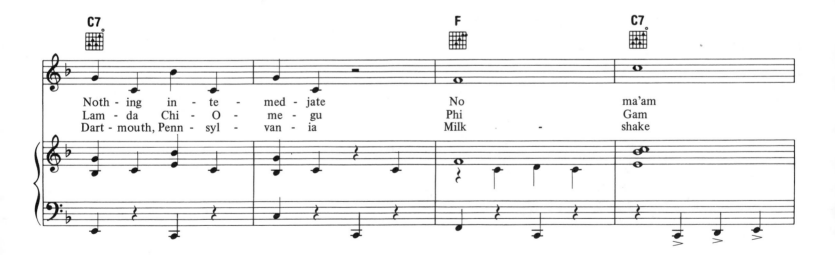

Noth - ing in - te - med - iate   No   ma'am
Lam - da Chi - O - me - gu   Phi   Gam
Dart - mouth, Penn - syl - van - ia   Milk - shake

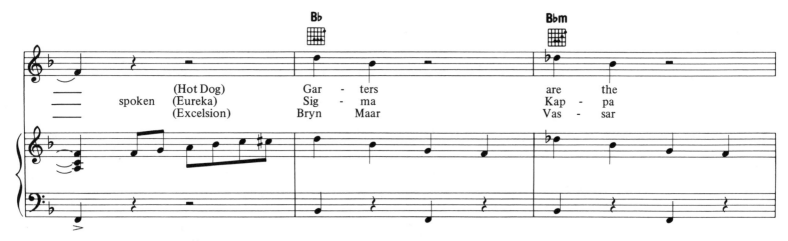

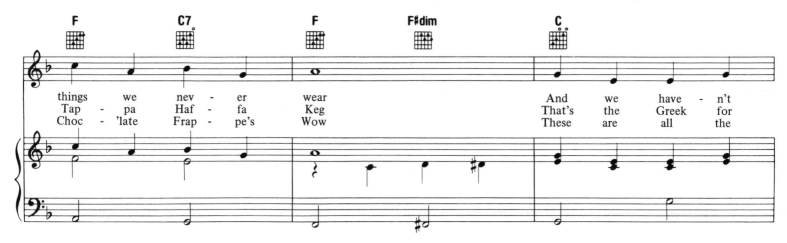

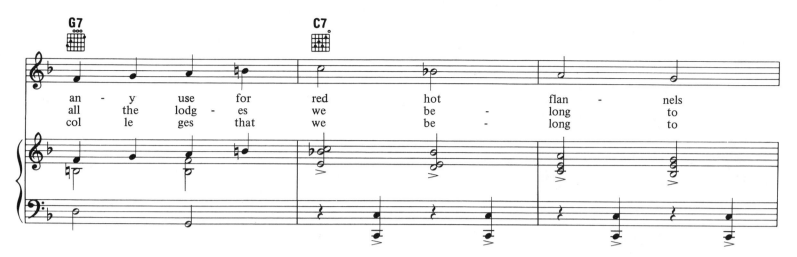

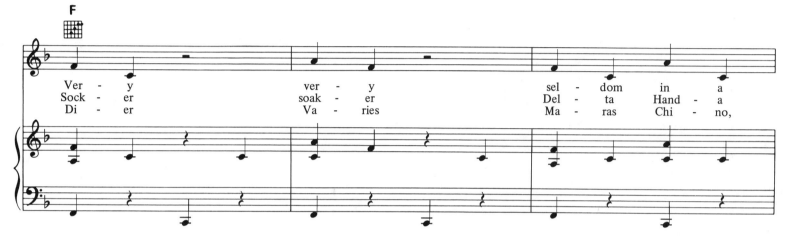

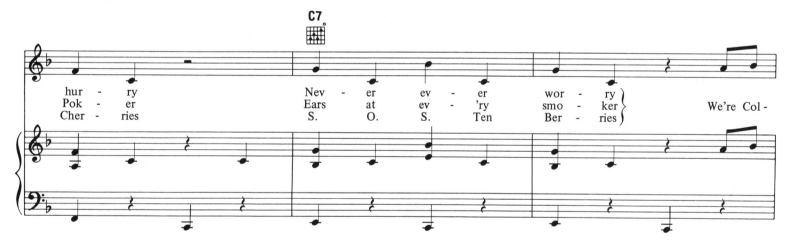

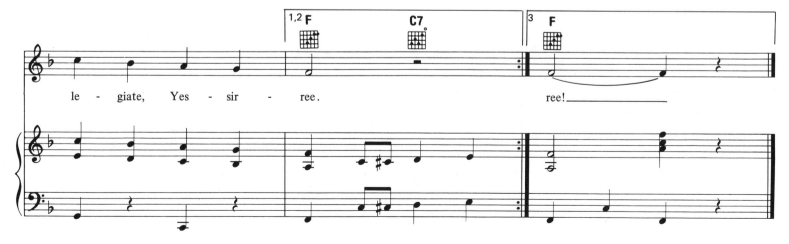

CHICKERY CHICK

Words by SYLVIA DEE
Music by SIDNEY LIPPMAN

Slowly (with an emphatic lift)

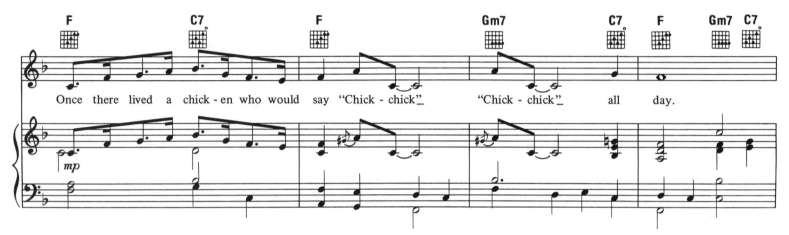

Once there lived a chick-en who would say "Chick-chick" "Chick-chick" all day.

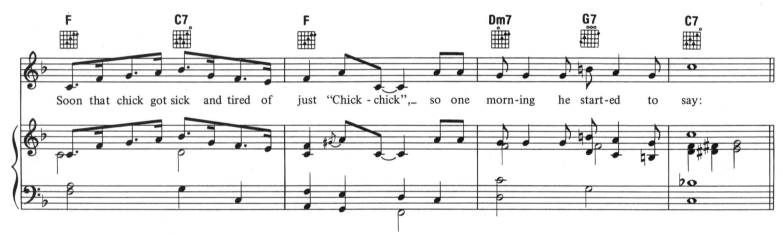

Soon that chick got sick and tired of just "Chick-chick", so one morn-ing he start-ed to say:

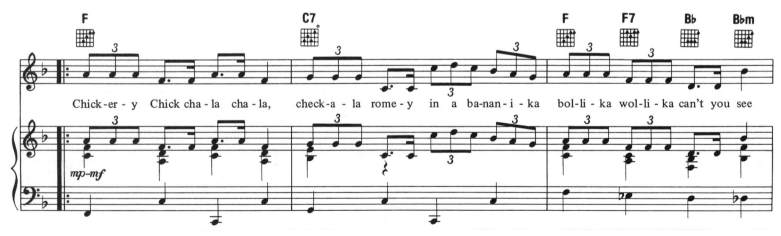

Chick-er-y Chick cha-la cha-la, check-a-la rome-y in a ba-nan-i-ka bol-li-ka wol-li-ka can't you see

CHIQUITA BANANA

Words and Music by LEN MacKENZIE,
GARTH MONTGOMERY and WILLIAM WIRGES

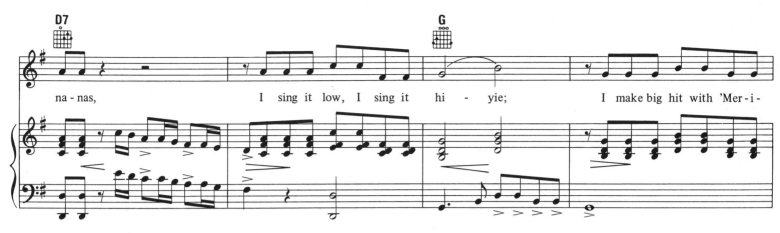

na - nas, I sing it low, I sing it hi - yie; I make big hit with 'Mer - i -

can - os, sing - ing song a - bout ba - na - nos. I could sing a - bout the moon - light on the

ver - y ver - y trop - i - cal E - qua - tor, But no, I sing a - bout ba -

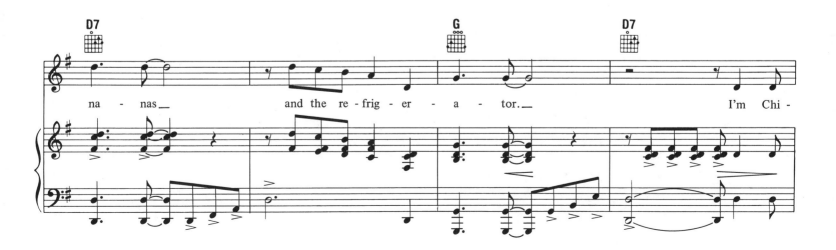

na - nas and the re - frig - er - a - tor. I'm Chi -

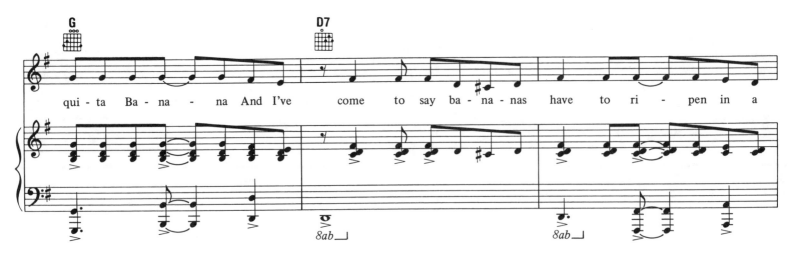

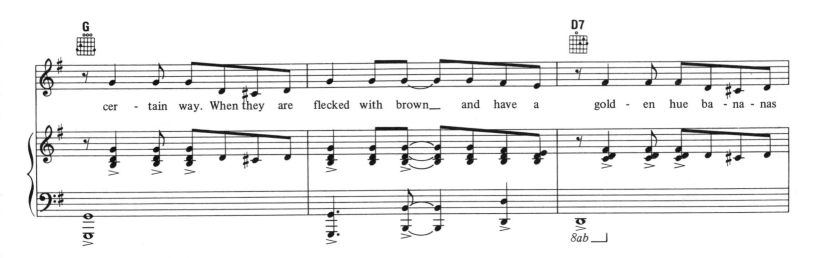

an - y way you want to eat them, It's im - poss - i - ble to

beat them; But ba - na - nas like the cli - mate of the ver - y ver - y trop - i - cal E -

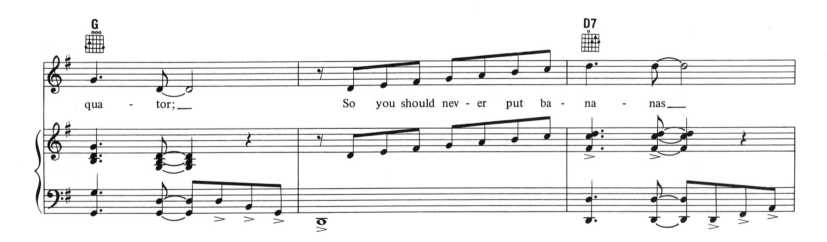

qua - tor;___ So you should nev - er put ba - na - nas___

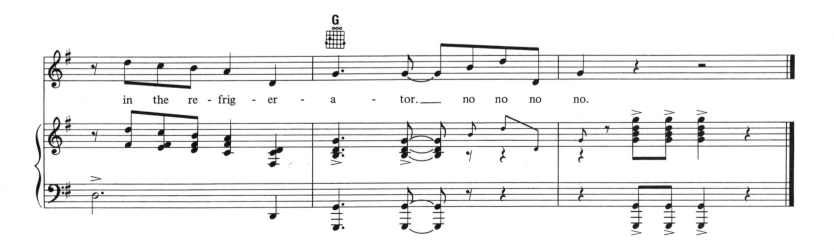

in the re - frig - er - a - tor.___ no no no no.

DANCE LITTLE BIRD

By TERRY RANDALL
and WERNER THOMAS

Rhythmically

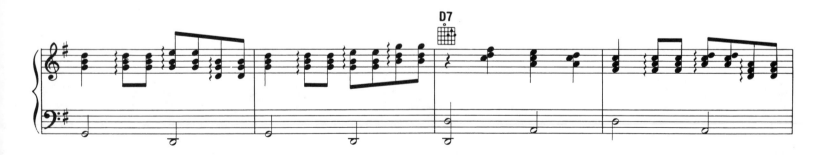

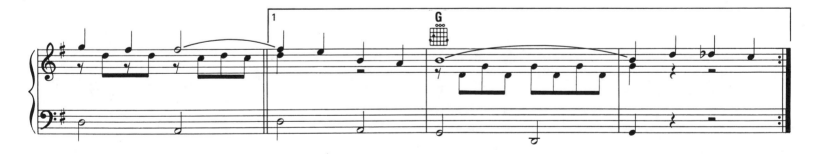

DUMMY SONG
(I'LL TAKE THE LEGS FROM SOME OLD TABLE)

Words and Music by LEW BROWN,
BILLY ROSE and RAY HENDERSON

GILLY GILLY OSSENFEFFER KATZENELLEN BOGEN BY THE SEA

Words and Music by AL HOFFMAN
and DICK MANNING

Flowing

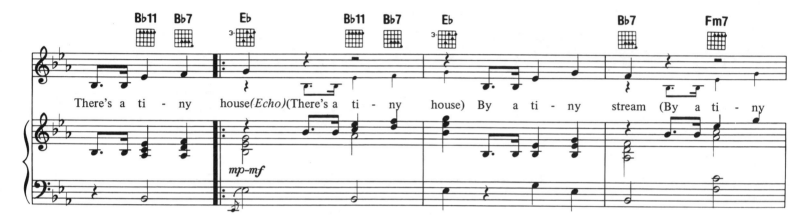

There's a ti - ny house (Echo) (There's a ti - ny house) By a ti - ny stream (By a ti - ny

stream) Where a love - ly lass (Where a love - ly lass) Had a love - ly dream (Had a love - ly

dream) And her dream came true (And her dream came true) Quite un - ex - pect - ed - ly__

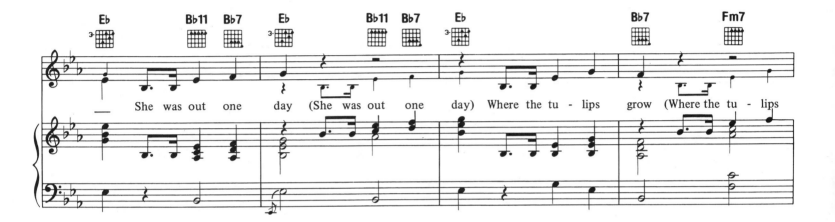

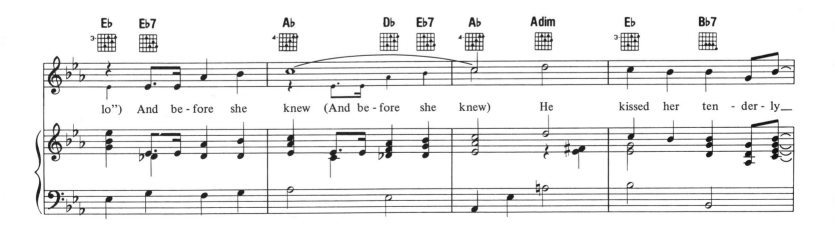

In Gil - ly Gil - ly Os - sen-fef - fer Katz - en - el - len Bog - en By The Sea

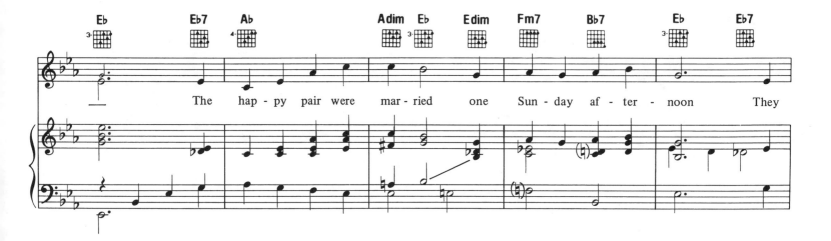

The hap - py pair were mar - ried one Sun - day af - ter - noon They

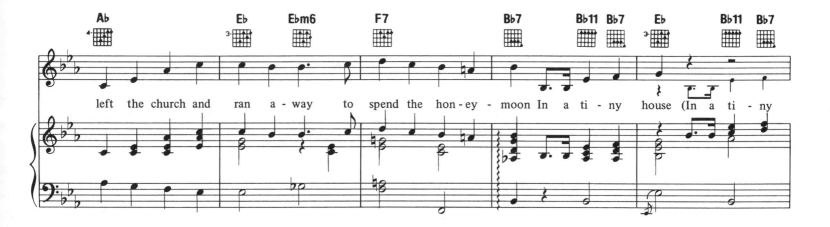

left the church and ran a - way to spend the hon - ey - moon In a ti - ny house (In a ti - ny

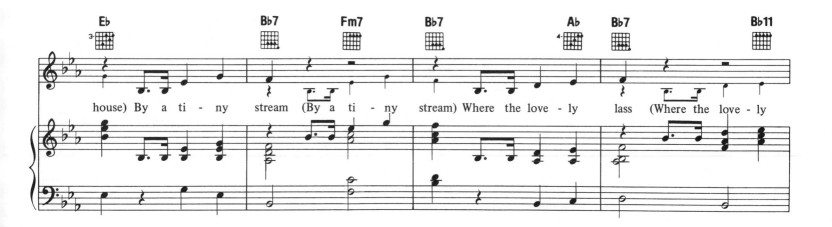

house) By a ti - ny stream (By a ti - ny stream) Where the love - ly lass (Where the love - ly

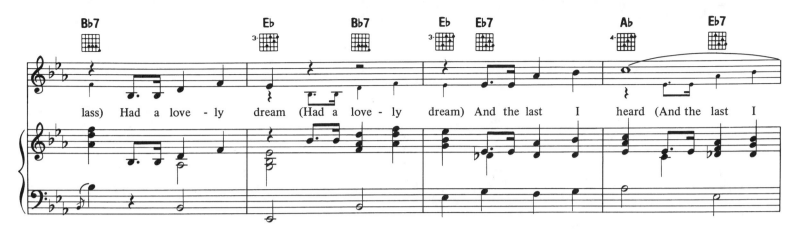

lass) Had a love-ly dream (Had a love-ly dream) And the last I heard (And the last I

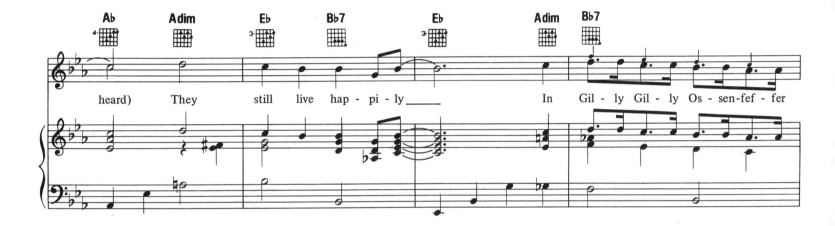

heard) They still live hap-pi-ly _____ In Gil-ly Gil-ly Os-sen-fef-fer

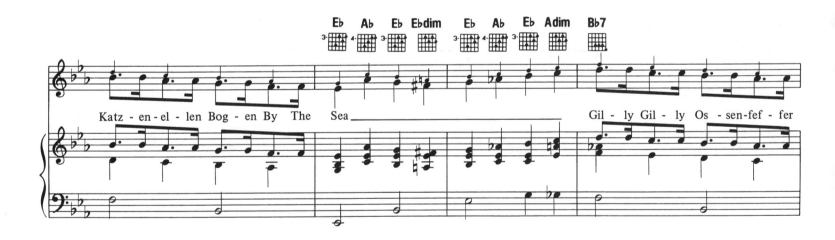

Katz-en-el-len Bog-en By The Sea _____ Gil-ly Gil-ly Os-sen-fef-fer

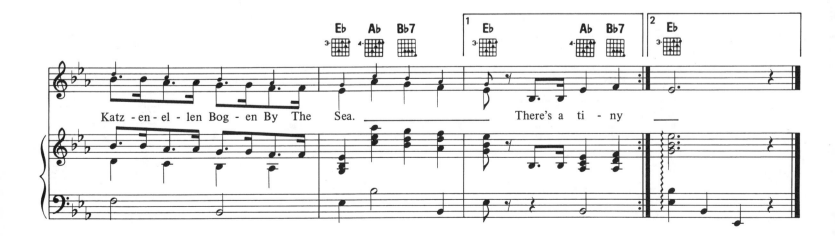

Katz-en-el-len Bog-en By The Sea. _____ There's a ti-ny _____

HELLO MUDDUH, HELLO FADDUH!
(A LETTER FROM CAMP)

Words by ALLAN SHERMAN
Music by LOU BUSCH

Medium Tempo

Hel - lo Mud - duh,   Hel - lo Fad - duh,   Here I am at   Camp Gra - al - li -
coun-s'lors.   hate the wait - ers,

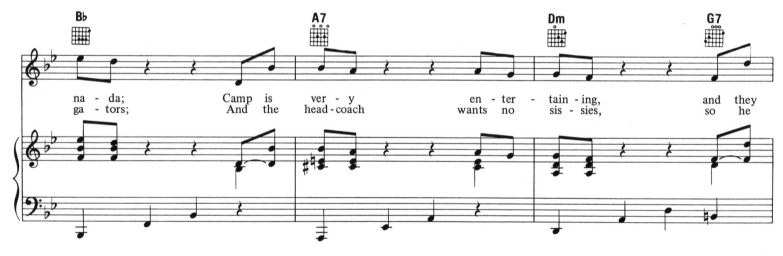

na - da;   Camp is ver - y   en - ter - tain - ing,   and they
ga - tors;   And the head-coach   wants no sis - sies,   so he

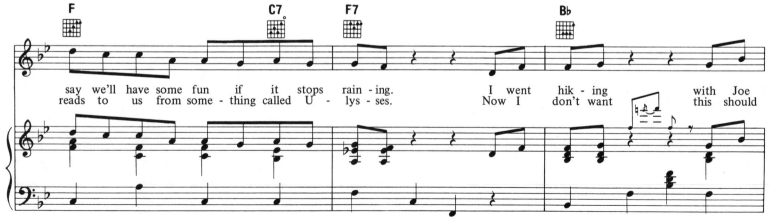

say we'll have some fun if it stops rain - ing.   I went hik - ing   with Joe
reads to us from some-thing called U - lys - ses.   Now I don't want   this should

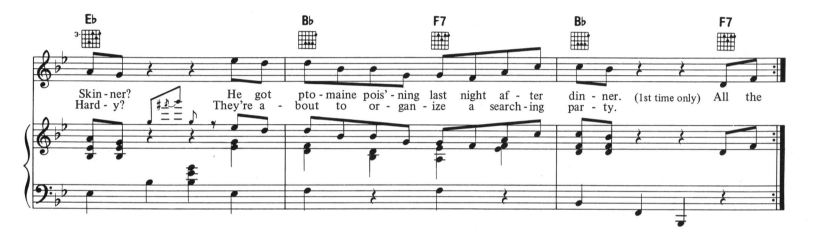

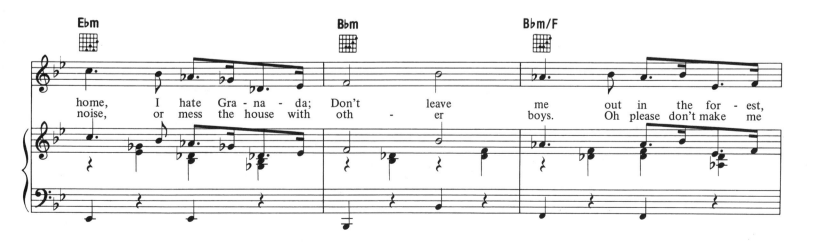

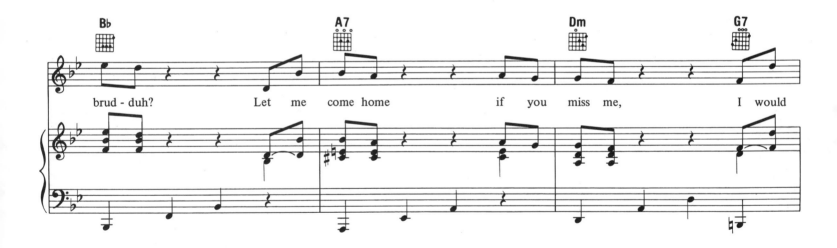

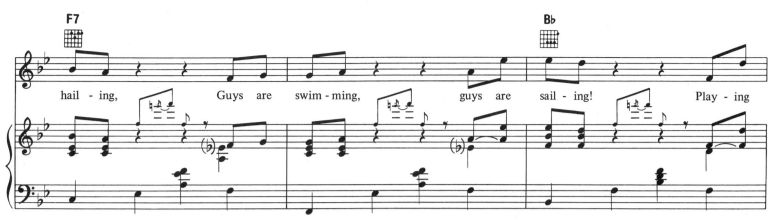

hail - ing, Guys are swim - ming, guys are sail - ing! Play - ing

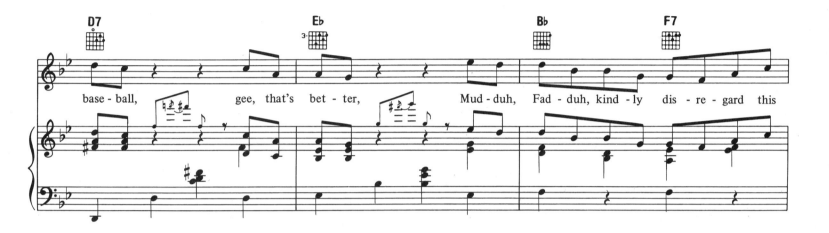

base - ball, gee, that's bet - ter, Mud - duh, Fad - duh, kind - ly dis - re - gard this

let - ter. Hel - lo

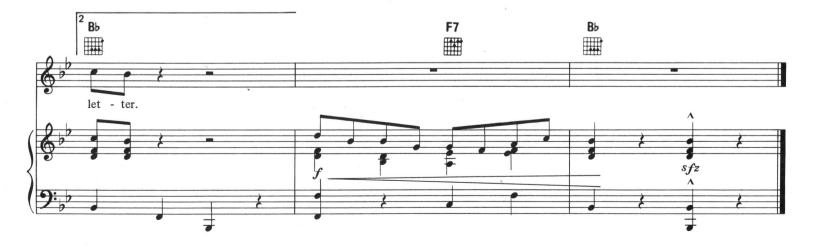

let - ter.

HONEY BUN
(From "SOUTH PACIFIC")

Words by OSCAR HAMMERSTEIN II
Music by RICHARD RODGERS

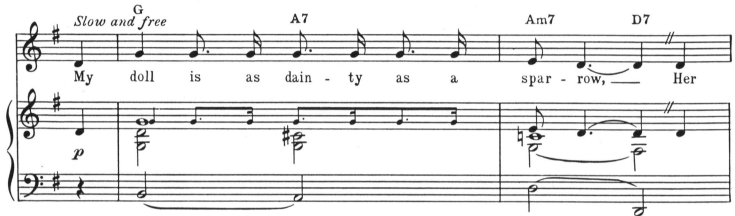

My doll is as dain-ty as a spar-row, ____ Her

fig-ure is some-thing to ap-plaud. Where she's nar-row she's nar-row as an

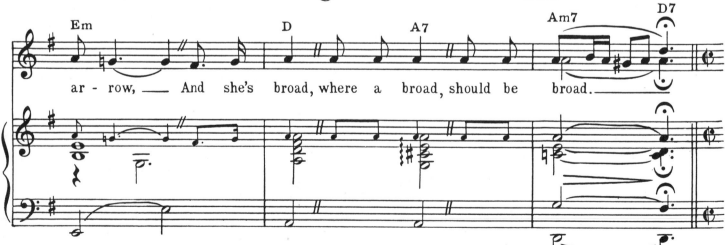

ar-row, ____ And she's broad, where a broad, should be broad. ____

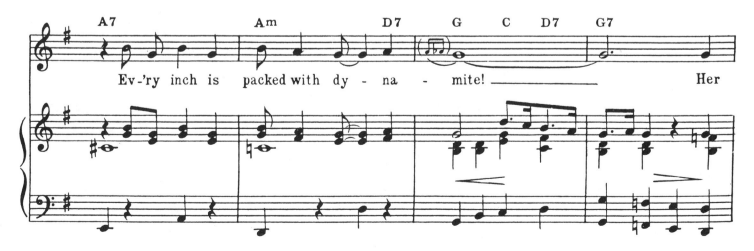

38

hair is blond and cur - ly, Her curls are hur - ly bur - ly. Her

lips are_ pips!_ I call her hips:_ "Twirl - y"_ and "Whirl - y."_

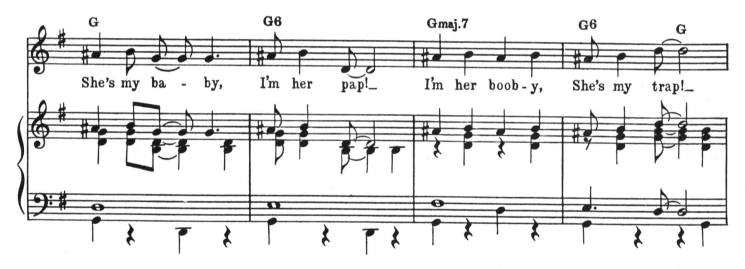

She's my ba - by, I'm her pap!_ I'm her boob - y, She's my trap!_

I am caught and I don't want-a run_ 'Cause I'm hav - in' so much fun with Hon - ey-

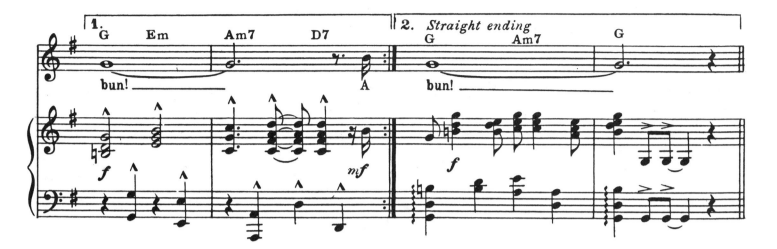

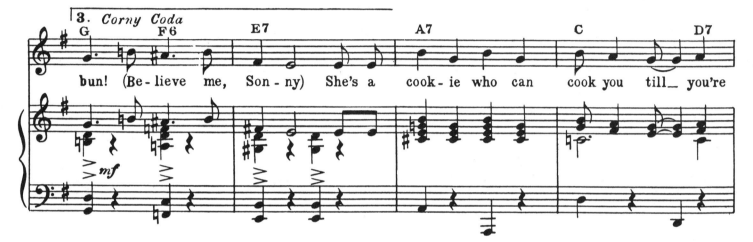

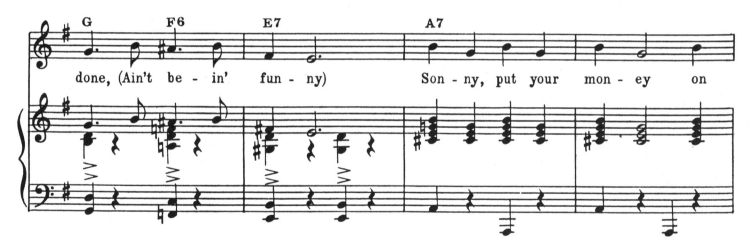

THE HUT-SUT SONG

Words and Music by LEO V. KILLION,
TED McMICHAEL and JACK OWENS

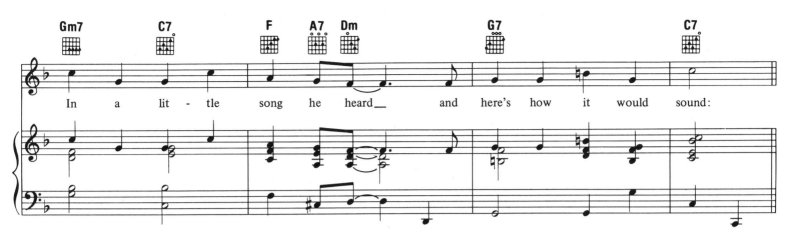

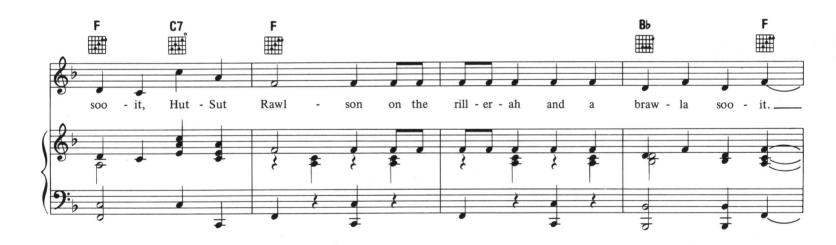

ITSY BITSY TEENIE WEENIE YELLOW POLKA DOT BIKINI

Words and Music by PAUL J. VANCE
and LEE POCKRISS

Brightly, with humor

She was a - fraid to come out of the

lock-er, She was as ner - vous as she___ could be; She was a - fraid to come out of the

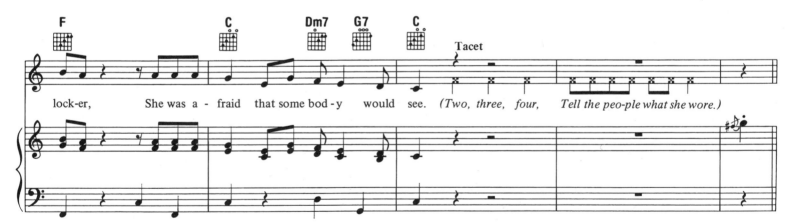

lock-er, She was a - fraid that some bod - y would see. *(Two, three, four,* *Tell the peo-ple what she wore.)*

It was an It - sy Bit - sy Tee - nie Wee - nie Yel - low Pol - ka-dot Bi - ki - ni,

That she wore for the first time to-day. An It-sy Bit-sy Tee-nie Wee-nie Yel-low Pol-ka-dot Bi-ki-ni,

So in the lock-er she want-ed to stay. *(Two, three, four, Stick a-round, we'll tell you more.* She was a-

fraid to come out in the o-pen, And so a blan-ket a-round her she wore; She was a-
fraid to come out of the wa-ter, And I won-der what she's gon-na do; Now she's a-

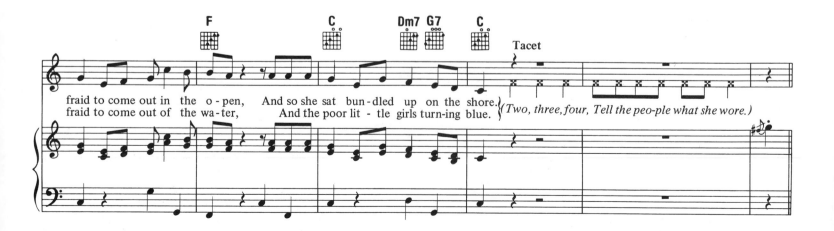

fraid to come out in the o-pen, And so she sat bun-dled up on the shore. } *(Two, three, four, Tell the peo-ple what she wore.)*
fraid to come out of the wa-ter, And the poor lit-tle girl's turn-ing blue.

I SCREAM-YOU SCREAM-WE ALL SCREAM FOR ICE CREAM

Words and Music by HOWARD JOHNSON,
BILLY MOLL and ROBERT KING

In the land of ice and snows Up a-mong the Es-ki-mos
Col-le-ges may come and go But the world will nev-er know

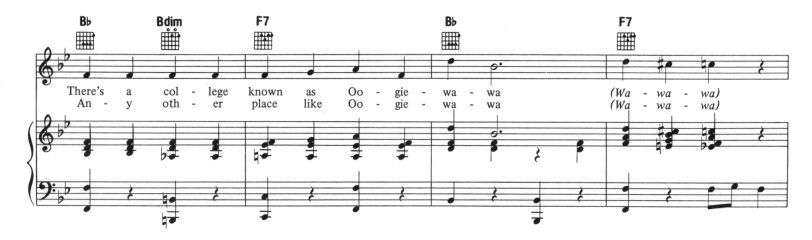

There's a col-lege known as Oo-gie-wa-wa (Wa-wa-wa)
An-y oth-er place like Oo-gie-wa-wa (Wa-wa-wa)

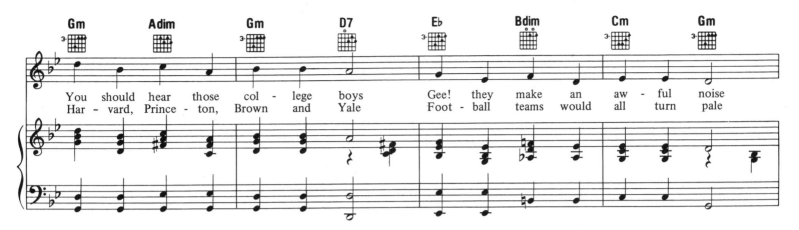

You should hear those col - lege boys Gee! they make an aw - ful noise
Har - vard, Prince - ton, Brown and Yale Foot - ball teams would all turn pale

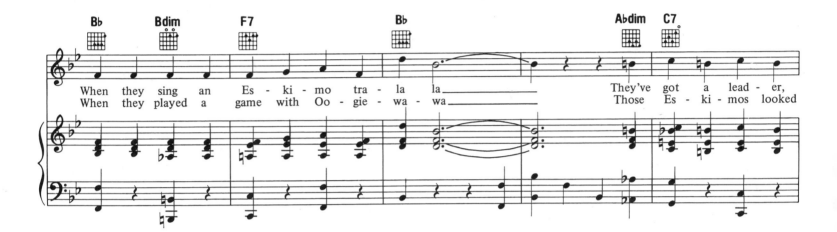

When they sing an Es - ki - mo tra - la la_____ They've got a lead - er,
When they played a game with Oo - gie - wa - wa_____ Those Es - ki - mos looked

big cheer lead - er, oh! what a guy___ He's got a fro - zen face, just like an
might - y tough when they took the field___ And peo - ple said "Ah!" there's a team that

Es - ki - mo pie___ When he says "Come on, let's go" Tho' it's for - ty-
nev - er will yield___ Then mid gore and fly - ing fur Just to show how

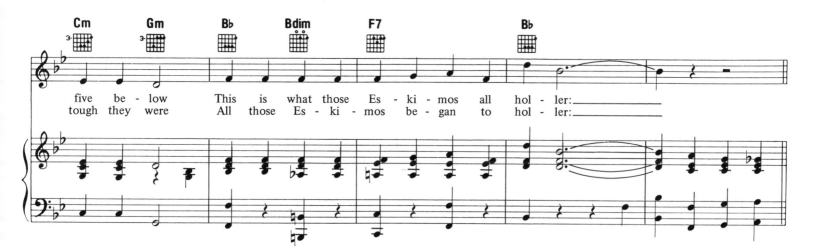

five be - low This is what those Es - ki - mos all hol - ler:_____
tough they were All those Es - ki - mos be - gan to hol - ler:_____

1. I Scream, You Scream, We All Scream For Ice Cream Rah!
2. I Scream, You Scream, We All Scream For Ice Cream Rah!
3. (Greek) Al - pha, Be - ta, A fro - zen to - may - tuh Yes!

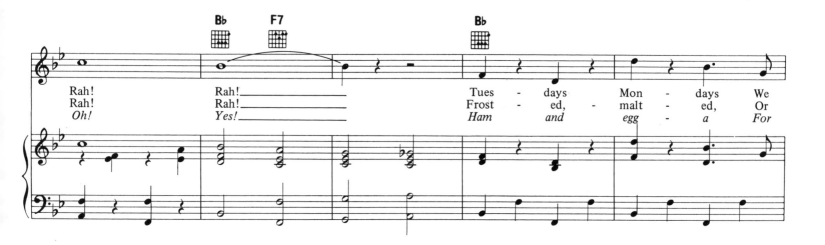

Rah! Rah! Tues - days Mon - days We
Rah! Rah! Frost - ed, - malt - ed, Or
Oh! Yes! Ham and egg a For

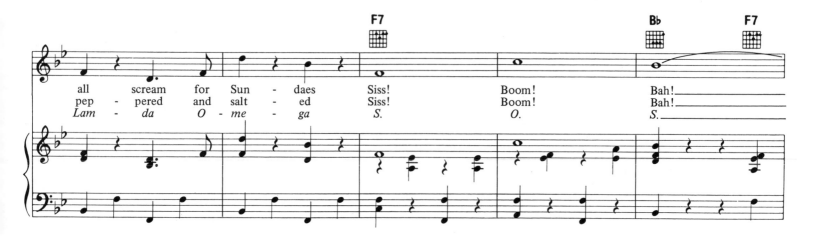

all scream for Sun - daes Siss! Boom! Bah!_____
pep - pered and salt - ed Siss! Boom! Bah!_____
Lam - da O - me - ga S. O. S._____

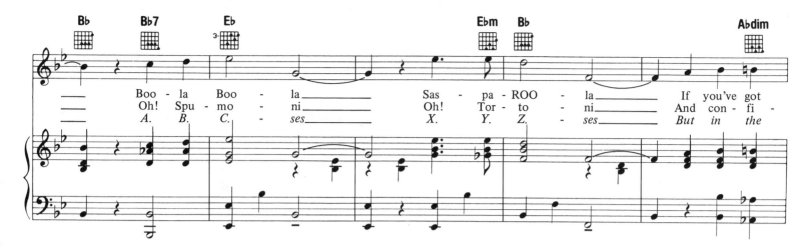

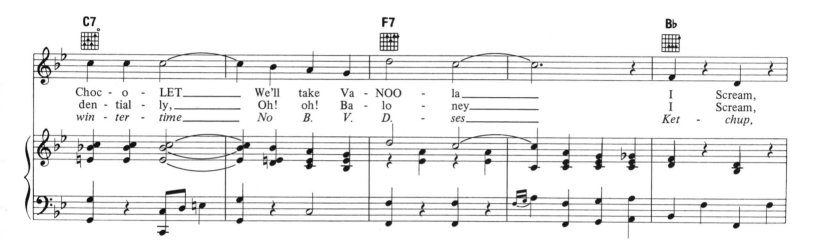

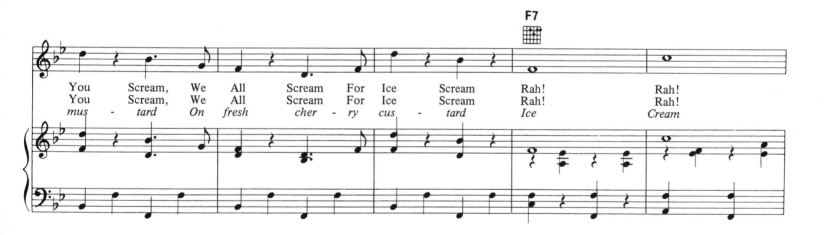

I'M A LONELY LITTLE PETUNIA
(In An Onion Patch)

Words by MAURIE HARTMANN and BILLY FABER
Music by MAURIE HARTMANN and JOHNNY KAMANO

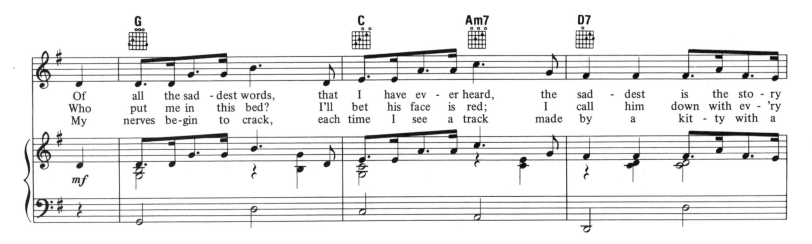

Of all the sad-dest words, that I have ev-er heard, the sad-dest is the sto-ry
Who put me in this bed? I'll bet his face is red; I call him down with ev-'ry
My nerves be-gin to crack, each time I see a track made by a kit-ty with a

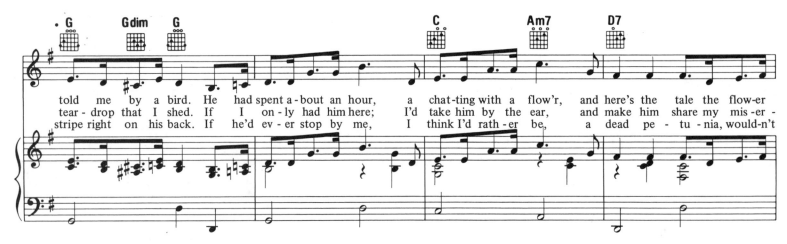

told me by a bird. He had spent a-bout an hour, a chat-ting with a flow'r, and here's the tale the flow-er
tear-drop that I shed. If I on-ly had him here; I'd take him by the ear, and make him share my mis-er-
stripe right on his back. If he'd ev-er stop by me, I think I'd rath-er be, a dead pe-tu-nia, would-n't

told. Oh!
y. Oh! I'm A Lone-ly Lit-tle Pe-tu-nia in an on-ion patch, an on-ion patch, an
you? Oh!

on - ion patch, I'm A Lone-ly Lit-tle Pe - tu - nia in an on - ion patch, and

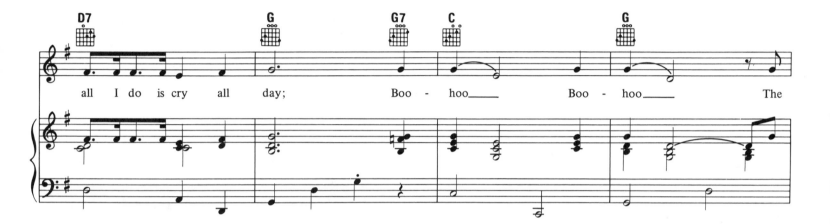

all I do is cry all day; Boo - hoo_____ Boo - hoo_____ The

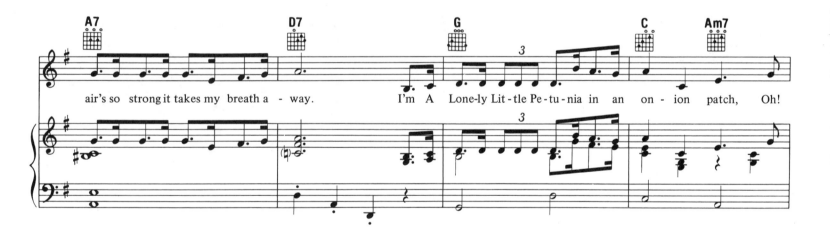

air's so strong it takes my breath a - way. I'm A Lone-ly Lit-tle Pe - tu - nia in an on - ion patch, Oh!

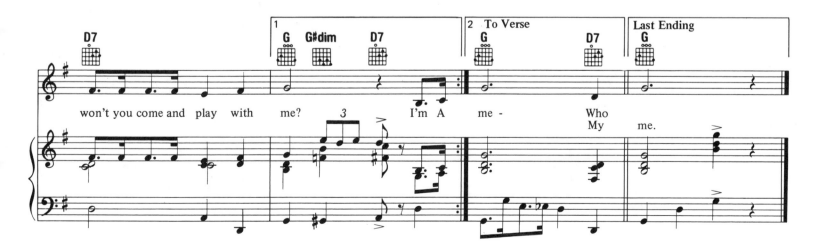

won't you come and play with me? I'm A me - Who
My me.

I'M LOOKING OVER A FOUR LEAF CLOVER

Words by MORT DIXON
Music by HARRY WOODS

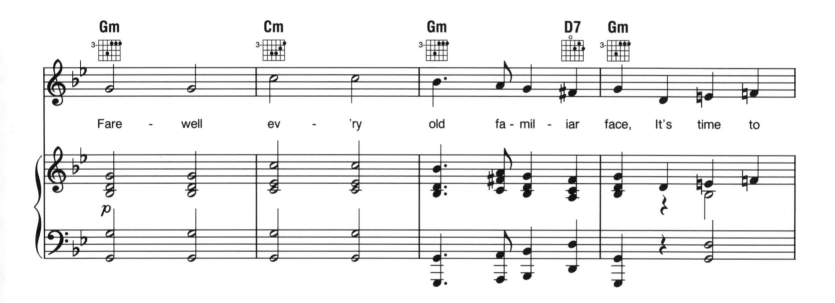

I'VE GOT A LOVELY BUNCH OF COCOANUTS

Moderately with spirit

Words and Music by FRED HEATHERTON

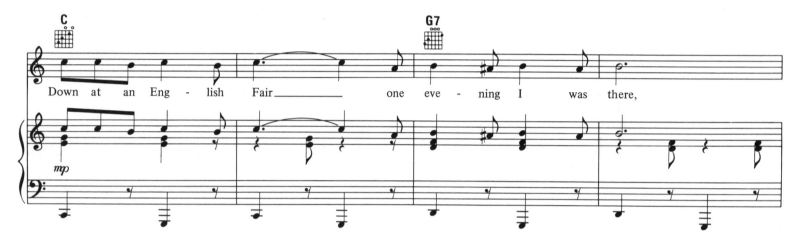

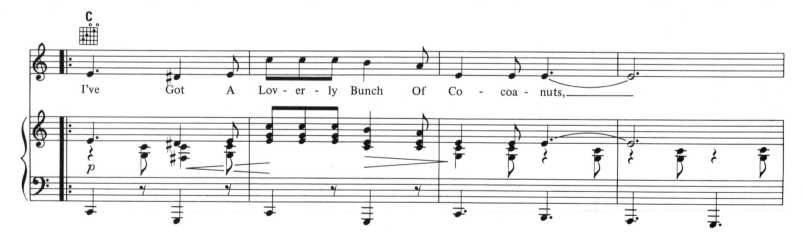

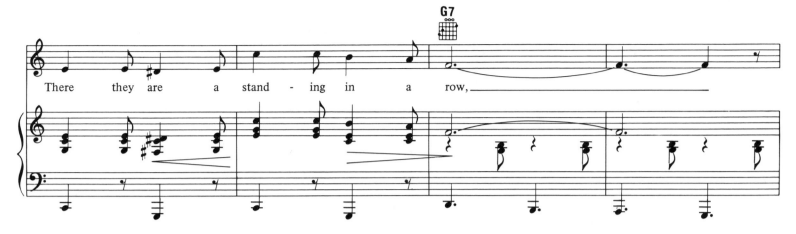

There they are a stand - ing in a row,_____

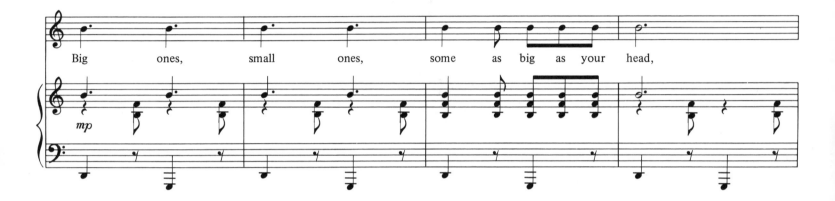

Big ones, small ones, some as big as your head,

Give 'em a twist, a flick of the wrist, That's what the show - man said.

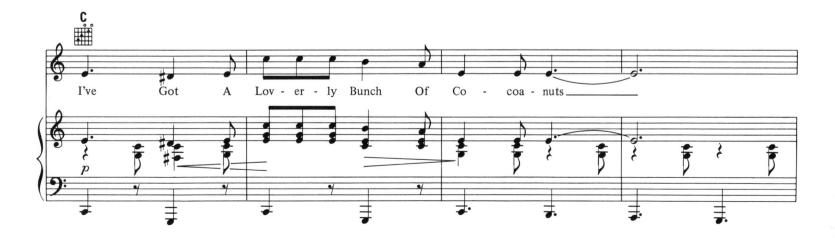

I've Got A Lov - er - ly Bunch Of Co - coa - nuts_____

Ev - e - ry ball you throw will make me rich;

There stands me wife,_____ The i - dol of me life, Sing - ing

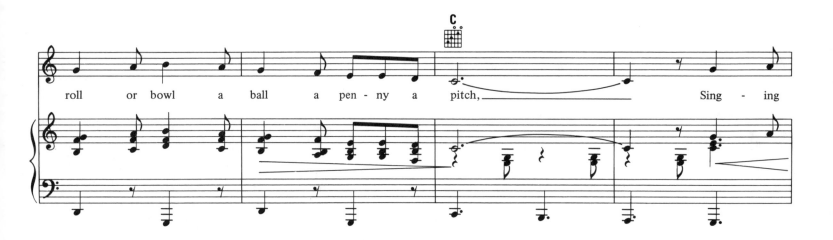

roll or bowl a ball a pen - ny a pitch,_____ Sing - ing

roll or bowl a ball a pen - ny a pitch,_____ Sing - ing

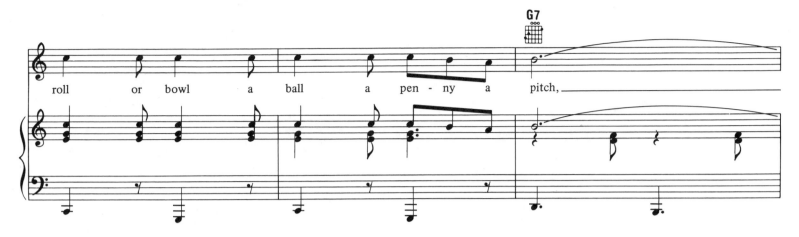

roll or bowl a ball a pen - ny a pitch,_____

____ Roll or bowl a ball, Roll or bowl a

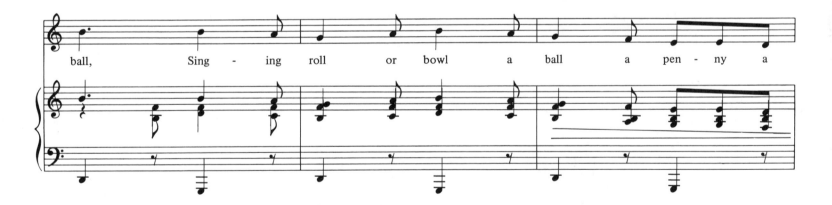

ball, Sing - ing roll or bowl a ball a pen - ny a

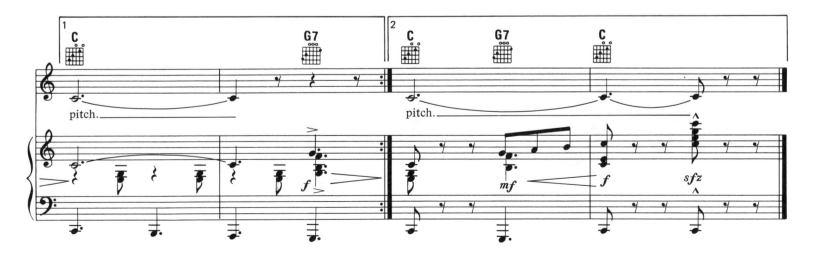

pitch._____   pitch._____

INKA DINKA DOO

Words and Music by JIMMIE DURANTE,
BEN RYAN and HARRY DONNELY

★) Letters over diagrams are names of
   the chords in original key and are
   adaptable to Banjo or Guitar.

What is that haunt-ing re-frain that you hear in the air?

Here and there, ev-'ry-where, It's just a

beau - ti - ful strain that keeps taunt-ing my brain con-stant - ly, _____ It's my mel - o -

dy _____ it's my sym-pho - ny. _____

CHORUS

INK - A DINK-A DOO, __ A dink-a dee, __ A dink-a

doo. Oh, what a tune _____ for croon - ing, _____

They've made their own Par - a - dise Land, Sing - ing

INK - A DINK-A DOO, ___ A dink - a dee, ___ A dink - a

doo, Sim - ply means INK - A DIN-KA DEE ___ A DIN-KA

DOO.

DOO. ___

LITTLE TIN BOX

Words and Music by JERRY BOCK
and SHELDON HARNICK

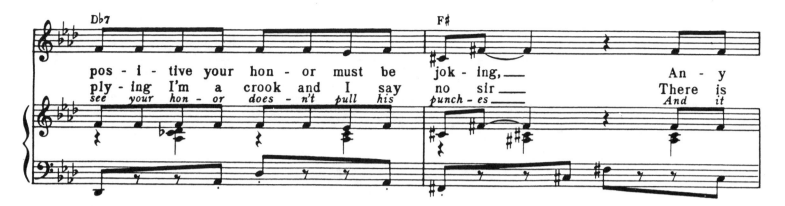

66

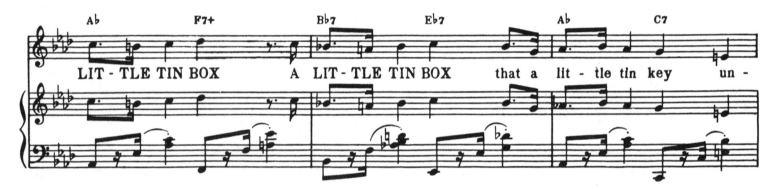

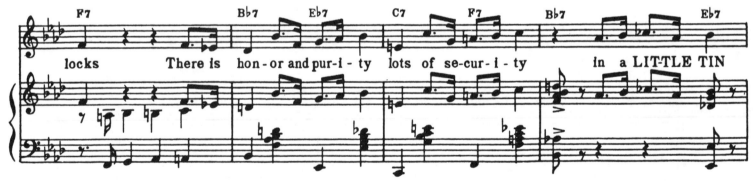

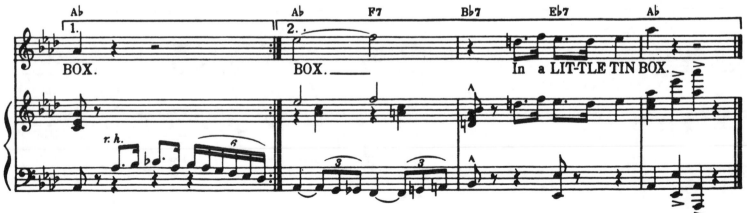

Lyrics For LITTLE TIN BOX

FOURTH HACK
Mr. "X," may we ask you a question?
It's amazing is it not?
That the city pays you slightly less
Than fifty bucks a week
Yet you've purchased a private yacht!

BEN
I am positive Your Honor must be joking
Any working man can do what I have done
For a month or two I simply gave up smoking
And I put my extra pennies one by one

Into a little tin box
A little tin box
That a little tin key unlocks
There is nothing unorthodox
About a little tin box

MEN
About a little tin box
About a little tin box

In a little tin box
A little tin box
That a little tin key unlocks

BEN
There is honor and purity

ALL
Lots of security
In a little tin box

FIFTH HACK *(Speaking)* Next witness.

FIRST HACK
Mr. "Y," we've been told You don't feel well
And we know you've lost your voice
But we wonder how you managed on the salary you make
To acquire a new Rolls Royce

BEN
You're implying I'm a crook and I say no sir!
There is nothing in my past I care to hide
I've been taking empty bottles to the grocer
And each nickel that I got was put aside

MEN
That he got was put aside

BEN
Into a little tin box
A little tin box
That a little tin key unlocks
There is nothing unorthodox
About a little tin box

MEN
About a little tin box
About a little tin box
In a little tin box
A little tin box
There's a cushion for life's rude shocks

BEN
There is faith, hope and charity

ALL
Hard-won prosperity
In a little tin box.

FIFTH HACK *(Speaking)* Next witness! Take the stand!

SIXTH HACK
Mr. "Z," you're a junior official
And your income's rather low
Yet you've kept a dozen women
In the very best hotels
Would you kindly explain, how so?

BEN
I can see Your Honor doesn't pull his punches
And it looks a trifle fishy, I'll admit
But for one whole week I went without my lunches
And it mounted up, Your Honor, bit by bit

MEN
Up Your Honor, bit by bit.
It's just a little tin box
A little tin box
That a little tin key unlocks

There is nothing unorthodox
About a little tin box
About a little tin box
In a little tin box
A little tin box
All a-glitter with blue chip stocks

BEN
There is something delectable

ALL
Almost respectable
In a little tin box
In a little tin box!

MAH-NA MAH-NA

By PIERO UMILIANI

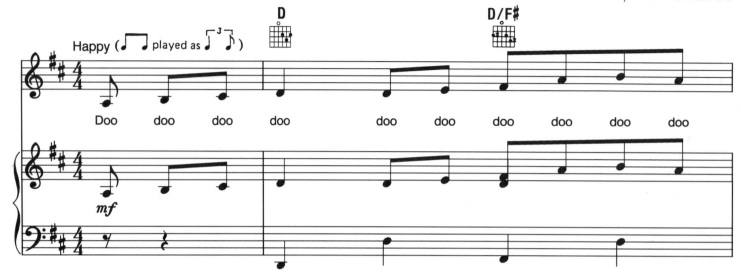

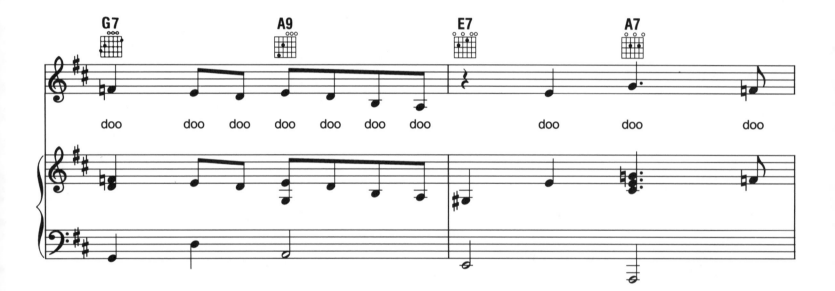

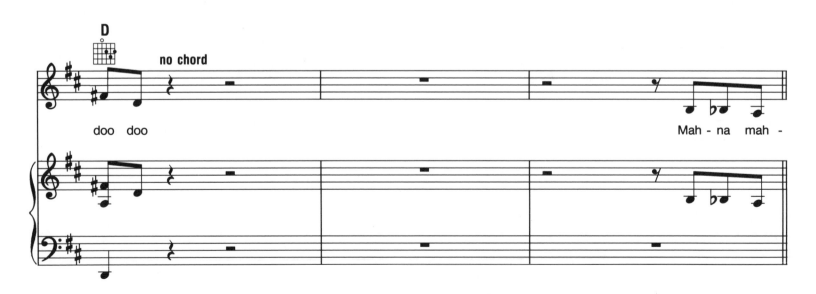

MAIRZY DOATS

By MILTON DRAKE, AL HOFFMAN,
and JERRY LIVINGSTON

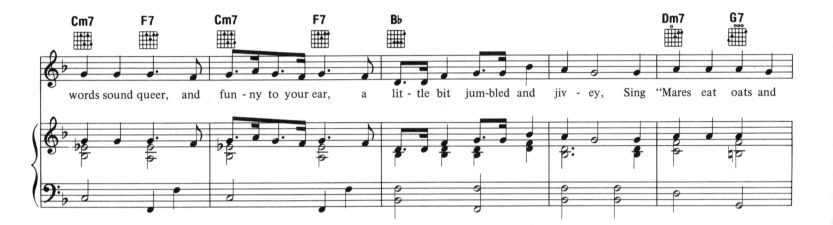

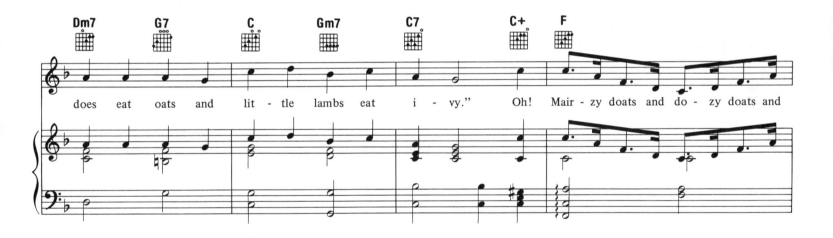

MONSTER MASH

Words and Music by BOBBY PICKETT
and LEONARD CAPIZZI

2. From my laboratory in the castle east.
To the master bedroom where the vampires feast.
The ghouls all came from their humble abodes
To catch a jolt from my electrodes.
(to Chorus: They did the mash)

3. The zombies were having fun,
The party had just begun.
The guests included Wolf-man,
Dracula, and his son.

4. The scene was rockin'; all were digging the sounds,
Igor on chains, backed by his baying hounds.
The coffin-bangers were about to arrive
With their vocal group "The Crypt-Kicker Five"
(to Chorus: They played the mash)

5. Out from his coffin, Drac's voice did ring;
Seems he was troubled by just one thing.
He opened the lid and shook his fist,
And said, "Whatever happened to my Transylvanian twist?"
(to Chorus: It's now the mash)

6. Now everything's cool, Drac's a part of the band
And my monster mash is the hit of the land.
For you, the living, this mash was meant too,
When you get to my door, tell them Boris sent you. (till fade)
(to Chorus: And you can mash)

MY ATTORNEY, BERNIE

Arranged for Piano by DAVID FRISHBERG

Words and Music by
DAVID FRISHBERG

Lyrics under the staff:

1. I'm im - pressed with my at - tor - ney Bern - ie
2. I'm in touch with my at - tor - ney Bern - ie
3. I ad - mire my at - tor - ney Bern - ie

- ie I'm im - pressed with his in - flu - en - tial
- ie In a clutch he can speed right to the
- ie I ad - mire an - y guy who knows his

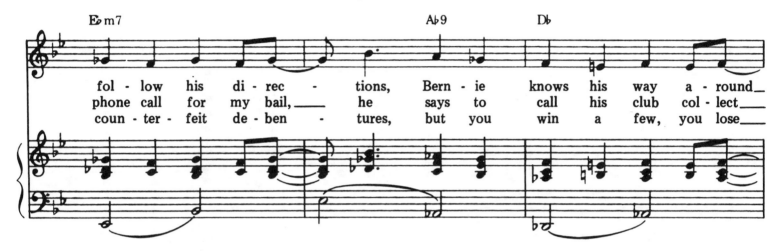

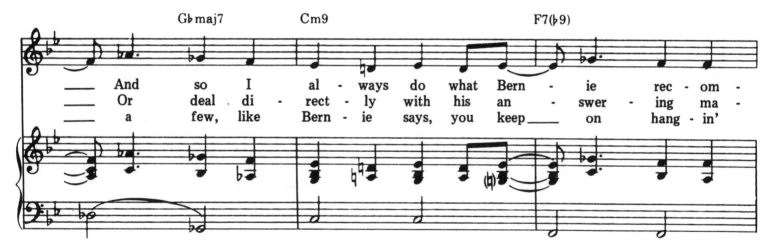

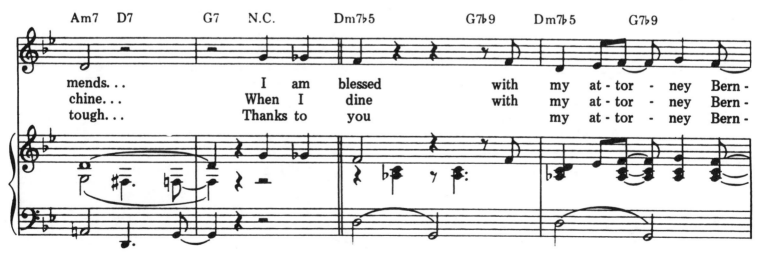

- ie, I'm im - pressed with the way he runs__ the
- ie, He buys wine from the rare im - port - ed
- ie, Thanks to you, I'm con - sid - ered well - to -

store... He's got Dodg - er sea - son box -
rack... That's 'cause Bern - ie is a pur -
do... Sure, I made out like a ban -

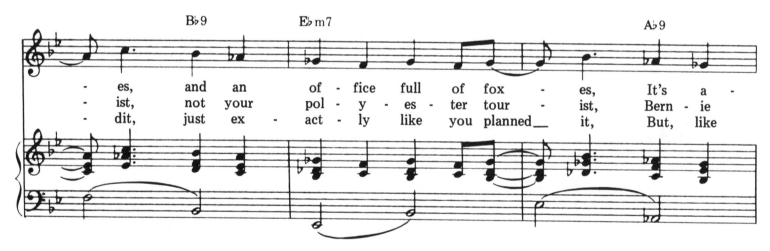

- es, and an of - fice full of fox - es, It's a -
- ist, not your pol - y - es - ter tour - ist, Bern - ie
- dit, just ex - act - ly like you planned__ it, But, like

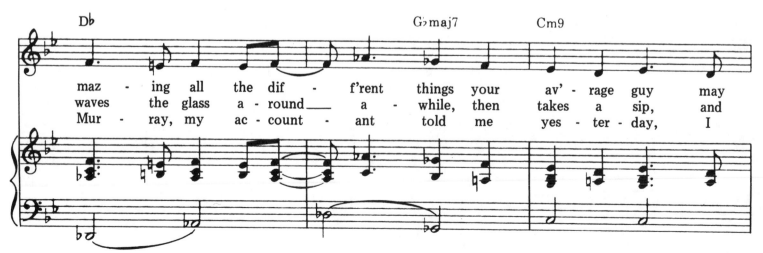

maz - ing all the dif - f'rent things your av' - rage guy may
waves the glass a - round__ a - while, then takes a sip, and
Mur - ray, my ac - count - ant told me yes - ter - day, I

NA NA HEY HEY KISS HIM GOODBYE

Words and Music by GARY DeCARLO,
PAUL LEKA and DALE FRASHUER

With a beat

1. Na na

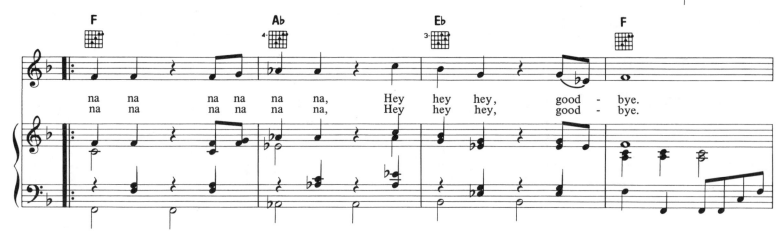

na na na na na na na, Hey hey hey, good - bye.
na na na na na na na, Hey hey hey hey, good - bye.

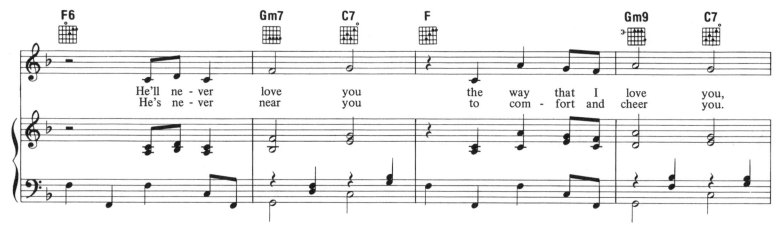

He'll ne - ver love you the way that I love you,
He's ne - ver near you to com - fort and cheer you.

'cause if he did no, no he would-n't make you cry. ___
When all those sad tears are ___ falling baby from your eyes. ___

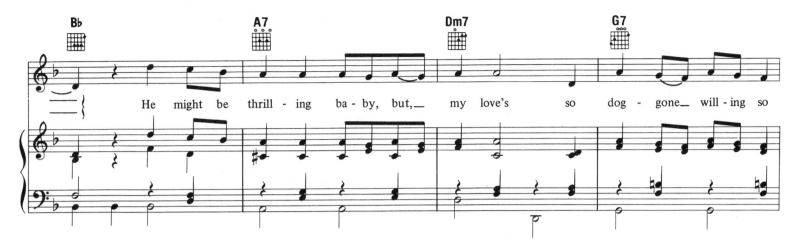

He might be thrill-ing ba-by, but,__ my love's so dog-gone__ will-ing so

kiss him,__ go on and kiss him good - bye. Na na

na na, Hey hey, hey, good - bye. Na na hey, hey good - bye. Na na

Repeat and Fade

na na na na na na, Hey hey hey, good - bye. Na na

OPEN THE DOOR, RICHARD!

Words by "DUSTY" FLETCHER and JOHN MASON
Music by JACK McVEA and DAN HOWELL

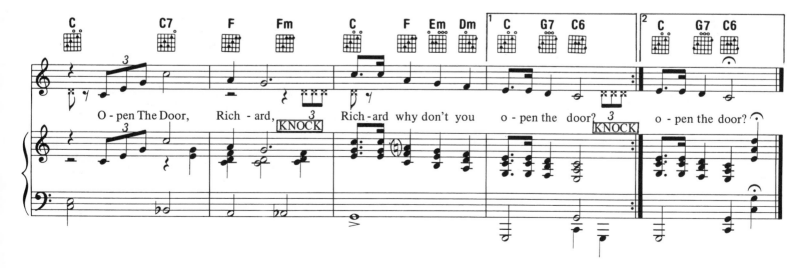

PADDLIN' MADELIN' HOME

Words and Music by
HARRY WOODS

Moderately

Verse

1. I love a girl named Ma-de-lin' I know she loves me, too For ev-'ry night the
2. The moon comes up at six o'-clock And I come up at eight She's al-ways wait-in'

moon is bright She rides in my ca-noe At mid-night on the ri-ver I
for my call And meets me at the gate I've pet-ted in the par-lor And

heard her fa-ther call But she don't care and I don't care If we get back at all:
hugged her in the hall But when she's out in my ca-noe I love her best of all:

Chorus

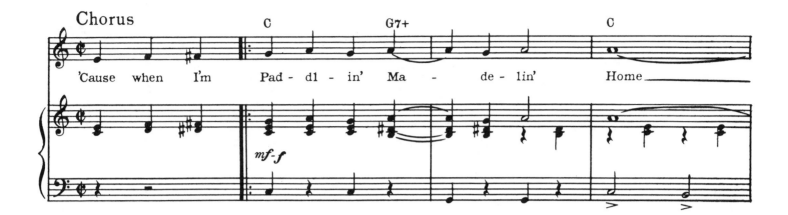

'Cause when I'm Pad - dl - in' Ma - de - lin' Home _____

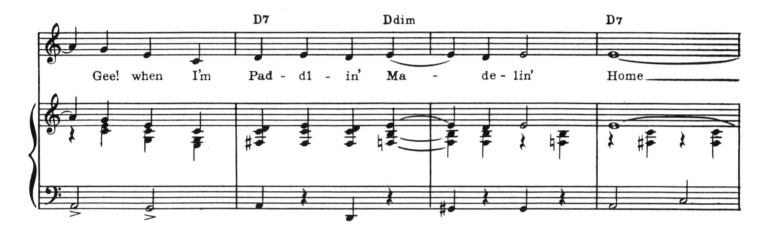

Gee! when I'm Pad - dl - in' Ma - de - lin' Home _____

— First I drift with the tide ____ Then pull for the shore ____
— First I kiss her a while ____ And when I get through ____

— I hug her and kiss ____ her and pad - dle some more ____
— I pad - dle for one ____ mile and drift back for two ____

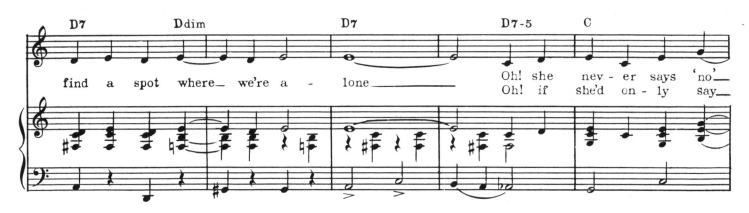

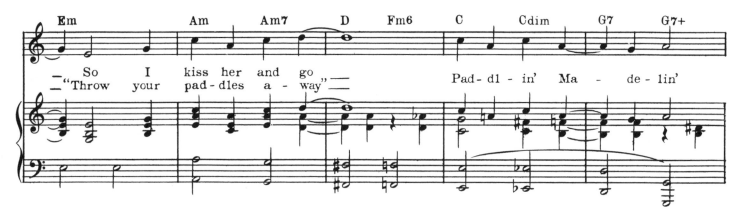

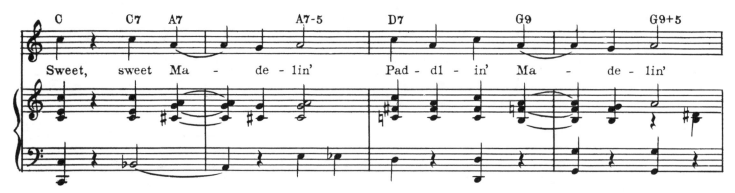

RAMA LAMA DING DONG

Words and Music by
GEORGE JONES, JR.

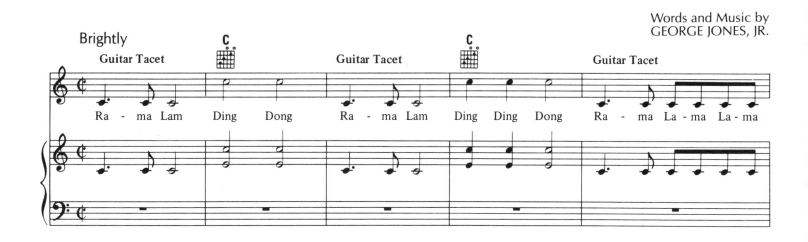

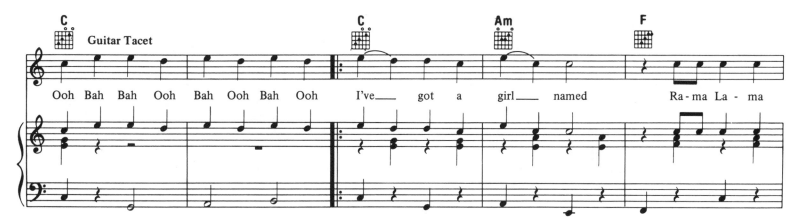

La-ma La-ma Ding Dong. She's ev - 'ry - thing to me, Ra - ma La - ma
She is fine to me,

La-ma La-ma Ding Dong. I'll nev - er set her free' 'Cos she's
You won't be - lieve That

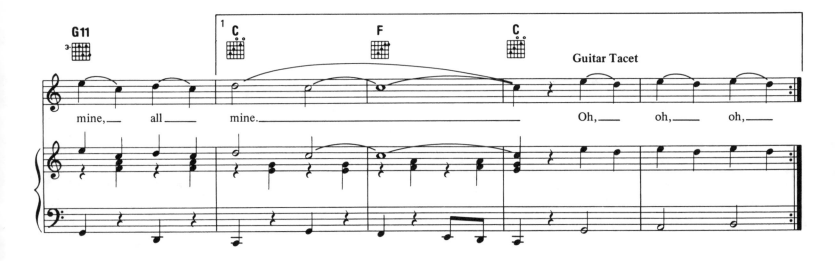

mine, all mine. Oh, oh, oh,

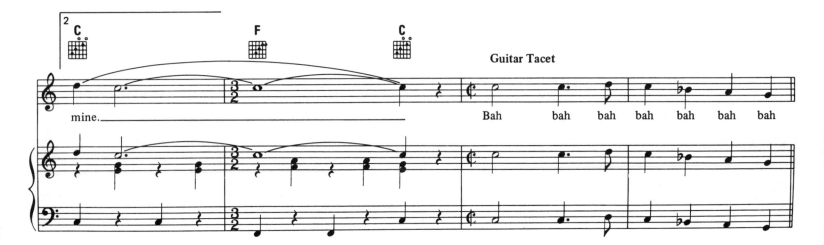

mine. Bah bah bah bah bah bah bah

bah. I love her, love her, love her so____ And now I'll

nev - er, nev - er let her go. One thing is cer - tain, she's

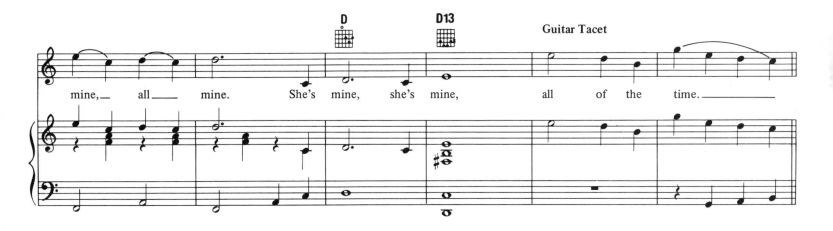

mine,__ all__ mine. She's mine, she's mine, all of the time._____

I've__ got a girl__ named Ra - ma La - ma La - ma La - ma Ding Dong. She's ev - 'ry -
2nd time instrumental

thing to me, Ra-ma La-ma La-ma La-ma Ding Dong. I'll nev-er set her free

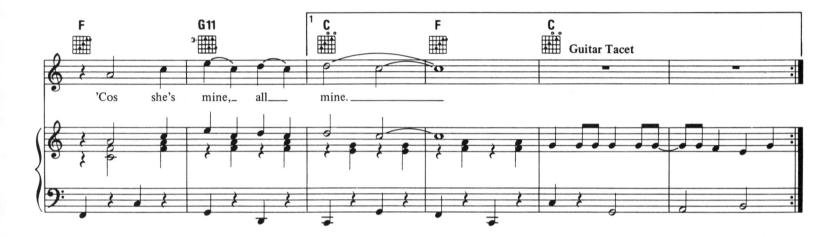

'Cos she's mine, all mine.

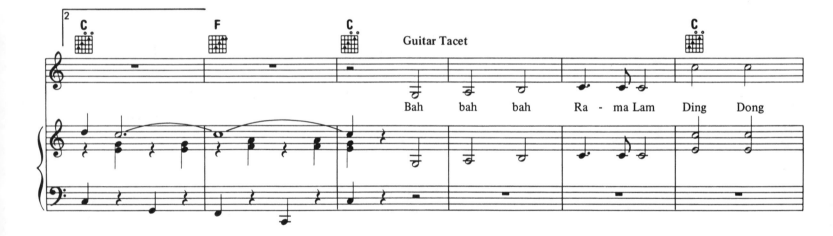

Bah bah bah Ra-ma Lam Ding Dong

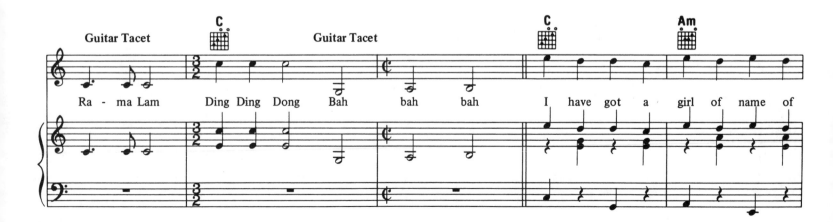

Ra-ma Lam Ding Ding Dong Bah bah bah I have got a girl of name of

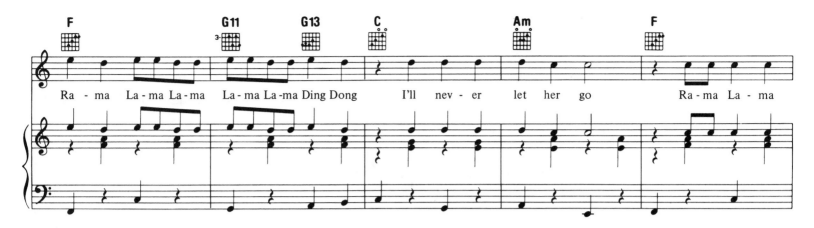

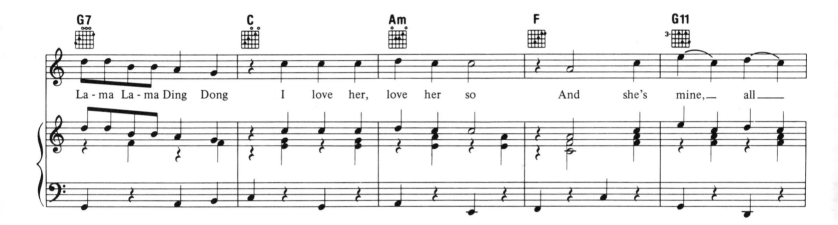

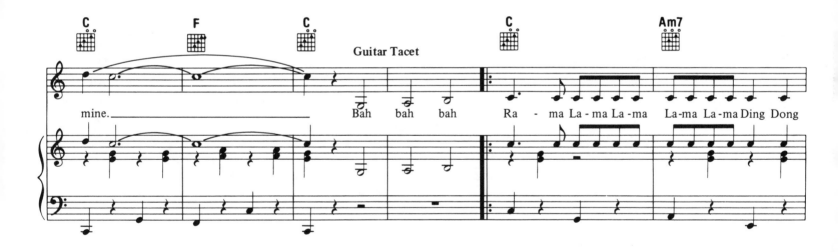

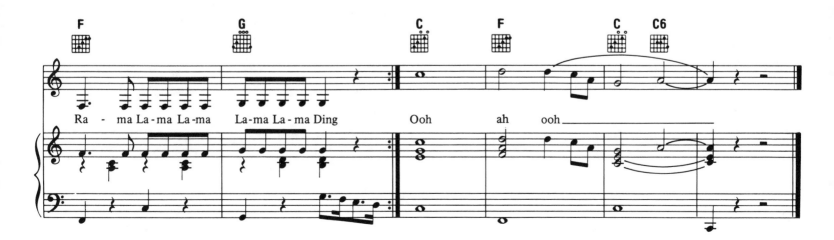

PURPLE PEOPLE EATER

Words and Music by SHEB WOOLEY

Bright rock tempo

Well, I saw the thing __ a - com - in' out of the sky, __ It had
Well, he came down to earth __ and he lit in a tree, __ I said,

one long horn and one big eye. __ I com - menced to shak - in' and I
"Mis - ter pur - ple peo - ple eat - er, don't eat me." __ I heard him say in a

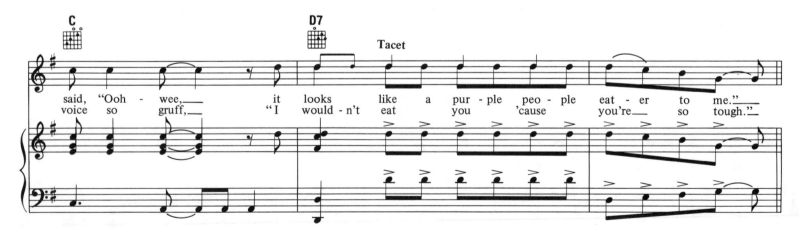

Tacet

said, "Ooh - wee, __ it looks like a pur - ple peo - ple eat - er to me." __
voice so gruff, __ "I would - n't eat you 'cause you're __ so tough."

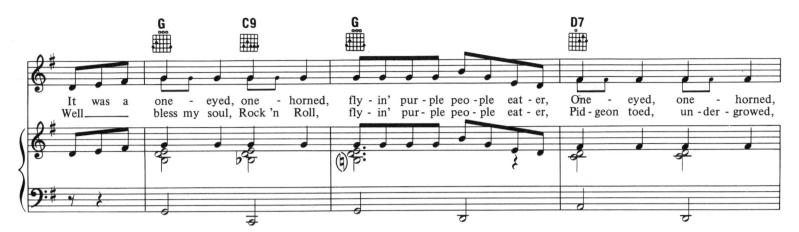

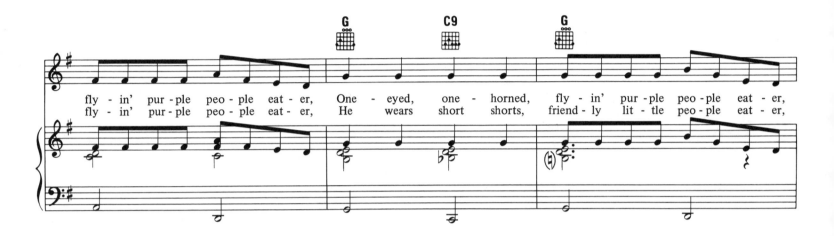

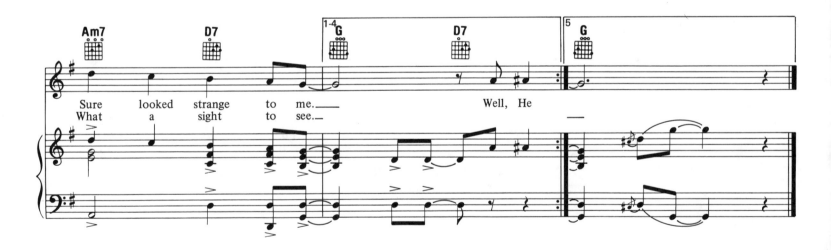

3. I said, "Mister purple people eater, what's your line?"
He said, "Eatin' purple people, and it sure is fine,
But that's not the reason that I came to land,
I wanna get a job in a rock and roll band."

4. And then he swung from the tree and he lit on the ground,
And he started to rock, a-really rockin' around.
It was a crazy ditty with a swingin' tune,
Singa bop bapa loop a lap a loom bam boom.

5. Well he went on his way and then what-a you know,
I saw him last night on a T.V. show,
He was blowin' it out, really knockin' 'em dead.
Playin' rock 'n' roll music thru the horn in his head.

RAG MOP

Words and Music by JOHNNIE LEE WILLS
and DEACON ANDERSON

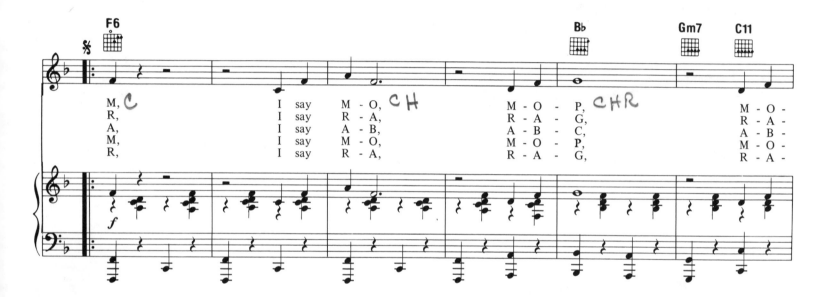

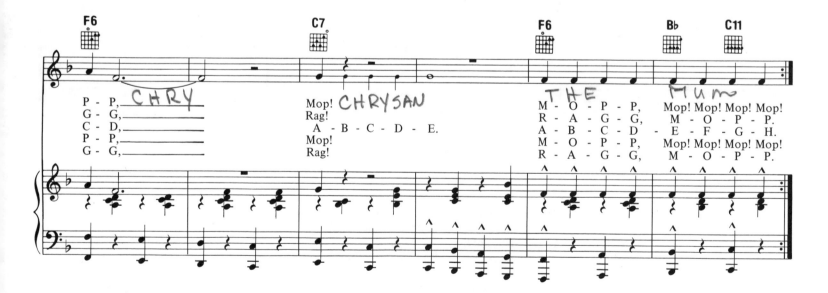

Chorus—*After 2nd and 5th Verses*

@hrysanthemun

Rag Mop! Rag Mop! Rag Mop!

Rag Mop! Rag Mop!

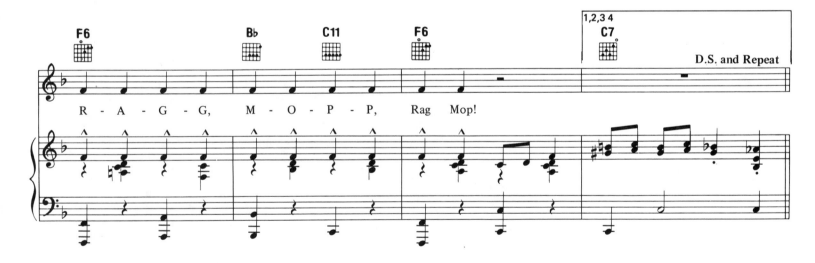

R - A - G - G, M - O - P - P, Rag Mop!

1,2,3 4

D.S. and Repeat

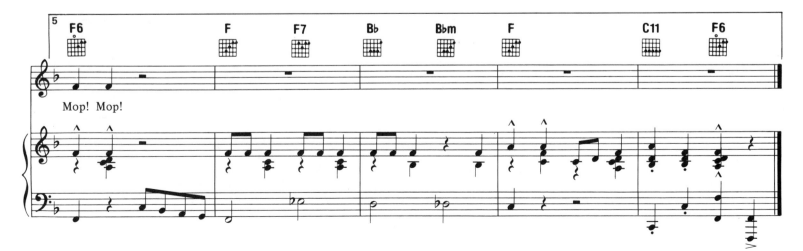

Mop! Mop!

5

SAM, YOU MADE THE PANTS TOO LONG

Words by FRED WHITEHOUSE and MILTON BERLE
Adapted from "Lord You Made The Night too Long"
by SAM M. LEWIS and VICTOR YOUNG

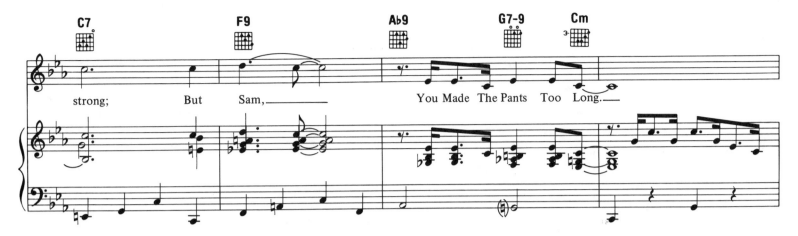

strong; But Sam,_____ You Made The Pants Too Long._____

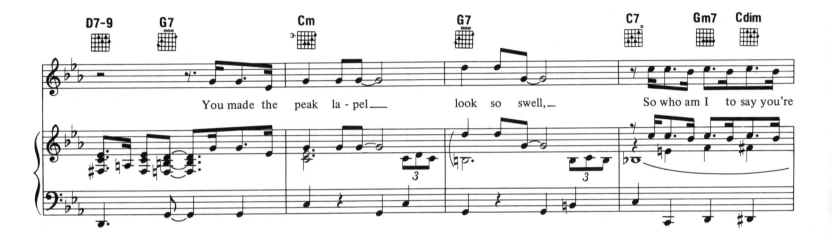

You made the peak la - pel____ look so swell,____ So who am I to say you're

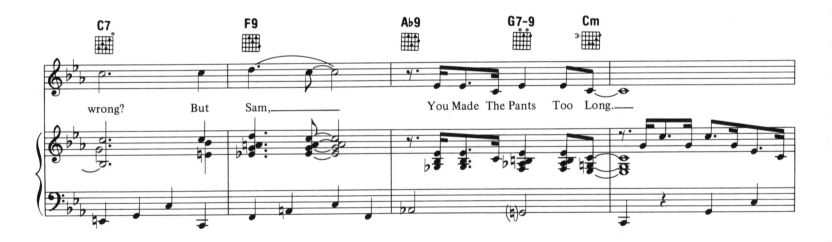

wrong? But Sam,_____ You Made The Pants Too Long._____

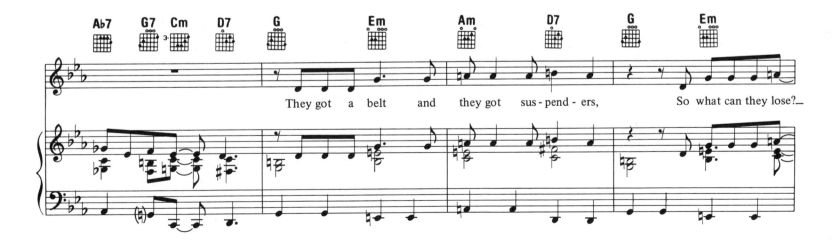

They got a belt and they got sus - pend - ers, So what can they lose?___

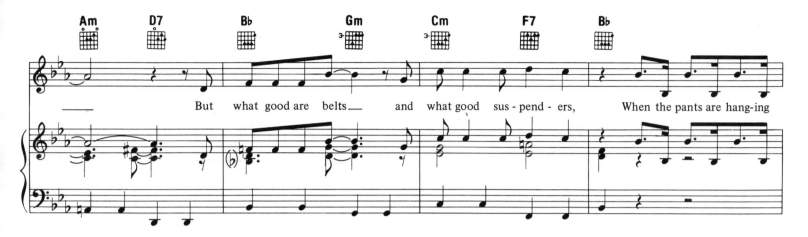

But what good are belts___ and what good sus-pend-ers, When the pants are hang-ing

o - ver the shoes.___ You feel a win-ter breeze___ up and down the knees, The belt is where the tie be -

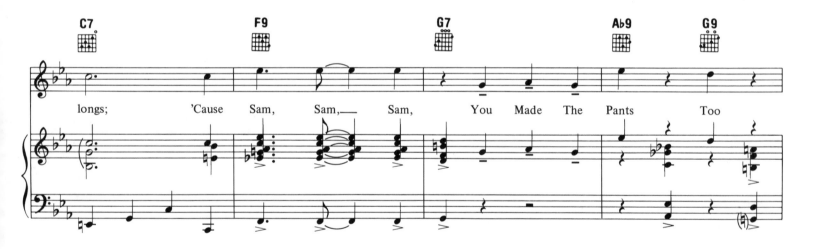

longs; 'Cause Sam, Sam,___ Sam, You Made The Pants Too

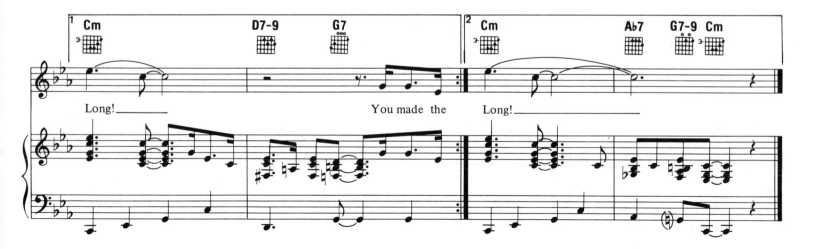

Long!_____ You made the Long!_____

SHOO FLY PIE AND APPLE PAN DOWDY

Words by SAMMY GALLOP
Music by GUY WOOD

Slow bounce

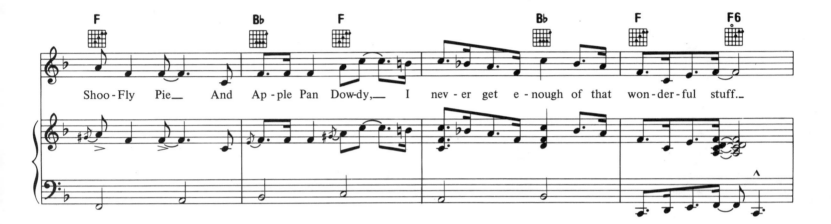

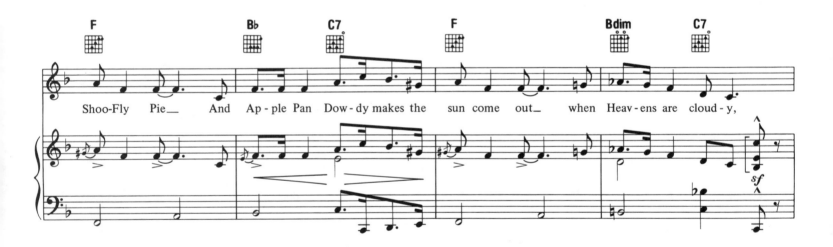

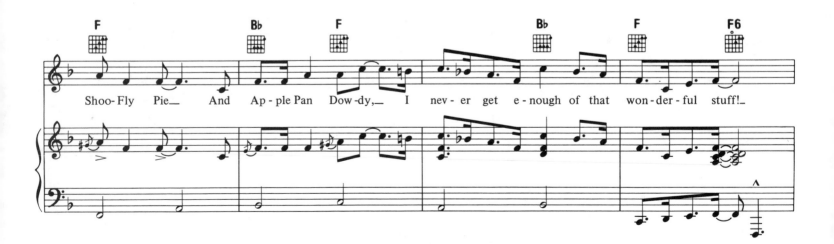

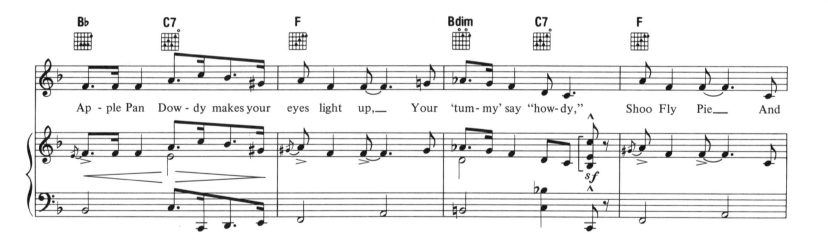

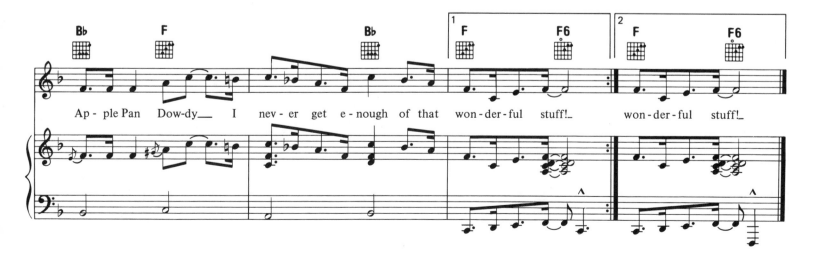

SUPERCALIFRAGILISTICEXPIALIDOCIOUS

(From Walt Disney's "MARY POPPINS")

Words and Music by RICHARD M. SHERMAN
and ROBERT B. SHERMAN

MARY POPPINS
Sup - er - cal - i - frag - il - is - tic - ex - pi - al - i - do - cious!

E - ven though the sound of it is some - thing quite a - tro - cious,

If you say it loud e - nough, you'll al - ways sound pre - co - cious.

SWEET VIOLETS

Words and Music by CY COBEN
and CHARLES GREAN

1. There once was a farm - er who
girl was told the farm - er that
farm - er de - cid - ed he'd

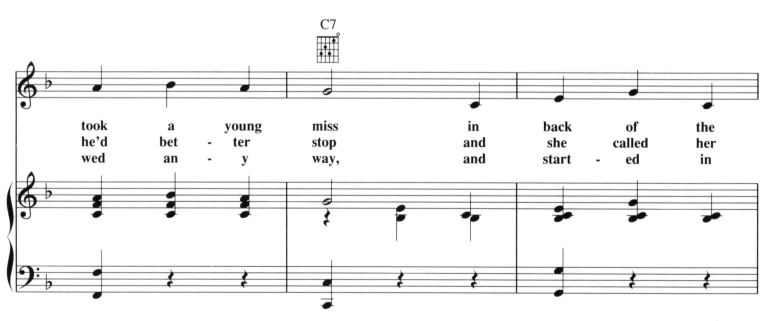

took a young miss in back of the
he'd bet - ter stop miss way, and back she called her
wed an - y way, and start - ed in

THE THING

Words and Music by
CHARLES R. GREAN

Moderately Bright

Chorus

1.While I was walk-ing down the beach one bright and sun-ny day,___ I
2. (I) picked it up and ran to town as hap-py as a king.___ I

saw a great big wood-en box a-float-in' in the bay.___ I
took it to a guy I know who'd buy most an-y-thing.___ But

pulled it in and o-pened it up and much to my sur-
this is what he hol-lered at me as I walked in his

prise,   Oh,   I dis-cov-ered a   *(Stamp Feet)*   Right be-fore my

shop: Oh, get out of here with that   Be - fore I call a

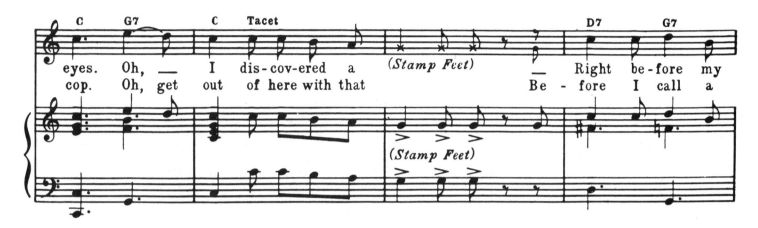

eyes.   Oh,   I dis-cov-ered a   *(Stamp Feet)*   Right be-fore my

cop.   Oh, get out of here with that   Be - fore I call a

eyes.   *(Vamp)*   2.I cop.

3) I turned around and got right out a-runnin' for my life,
And then I took it home with me to give it to my wife.
But this is what she hollered at me as I walked in the door:
Oh, get out of here with that xxx and don't come back no more.
Oh, get out of here with that xxx and don't come back no more.

4) I wandered all around the town until I chanced to meet
A hobo who was looking for a handout on the street.
He said he'd take most any old thing, he was a desperate man,
But when I showed him the xxx, he turned around and ran.
Oh, when I showed him the xxx, he turned around and ran.

5) I wandered on for many years, a victim of my fate,
Until one day I came upon Saint Peter at the gate.
And when I tried to take it inside he told me where to go:
Get out of here with that xxx and take it down below.
Oh, get out of here with that xxx and take it down below.

6) The moral of the story is if you're out on the beach
And you should see a great big box and it's within your reach,
Don't ever stop and open it up, that's my advice to you,
'Cause you'll never get rid of the xxx, no matter what you do.
Oh, you'll never get rid of the xxx, no matter what you do.

(Boop-Boop Dit-tem Dat-tem What-tem Chu!)
THREE LITTLE FISHIES
(Itty Bitty Poo)

Words and Music by
SAXIE DOWELL

Brightly

Down in the mead-ow in a lit-tle bit-ty pool, Swam three lit-tle fish-ies and a ma-ma fish-ie too,
Down in de med-dy in a IT - TY BIT- TY POO, Fam fee it - ty fit - ty and a ma-ma fit-ty, foo.
"Stop" said the ma-ma fish-ie "Or you will get lost," The three lit-tle fish-ies did - n't wan-na be bossed. The
"Top!" ted de ma-ma fit-ty "Or oo ill det ost," De fee it - ty fit-ty din na an-na be bossed. De

"Swim" said the ma-ma fish-ie, "Swim if you can," And they swam and they swam all o-ver the dam.
"Fim" fed de ma-ma fit-ty, "Fim if oo tan," And dey fam and dey fam all o-ver de dam.
three lit-tle fish-ies went off on a spree, And they swam and they swam right out to the sea.
fee it - ty fit-ty ent off on a spwee, And dey fam and dey fam ight out to de fee.

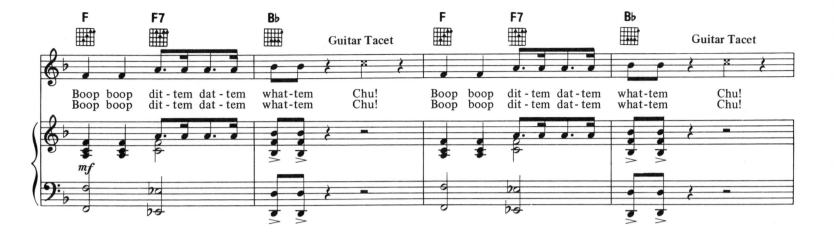

Interlude

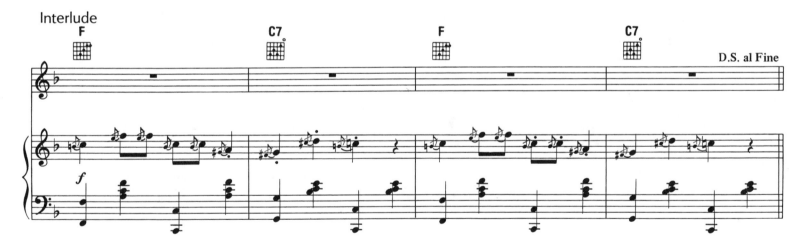

3rd Chorus

"Whee!" yelled the little fishies, "Here's a lot of fun,
We'll swim in the sea till the day is done."
They swam and they swam and it was a lark,
Till all of a sudden they met a SHARK!

("Whee!" 'elled de itty fitties "Ears a wot of fun,
Ee'll fim in de fee ill de day is un."
Dey fam and dey fam and it was a wark,
Till aw of a tudden dey taw a TARK!)

Boop boop dit-tem dot-tem what-tem Chu!
    "   "   "   "   "   "   "   "   "
    "   "   "   "   "   "   "   "   "
Till aw of a tudden dey taw a TARK!

4th Chorus

"Help!" cried the little fishies, "Gee! look at all the whales!"
And quick as they could they turned on their tails.
And back to the pool in the meadow they swam,
And they swam and they swam back over the dam.

("He'p!" tied de itty fitties, "Dee! ook at all de fales!"
And twit as dey tood dey turned on deir tails!
And bat to de poo in de meddy dey fam,
And dey fam and dey fam bat over de dam.)

Boop boop dit-tem dot-tem what-tem Chu!
    "   "   "   "   "   "   "   "   "
    "   "   "   "   "   "   "   "   "
And dey fam and dey fam bat over de dam.

TOO FAT POLKA

By ROSS MacLEAN and ARTHUR RICHARDSON

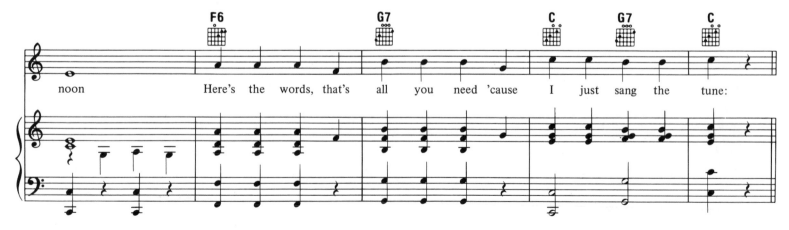

Chorus

Oh! I don't want her, you can have her, she's too fat for me She's too fat for

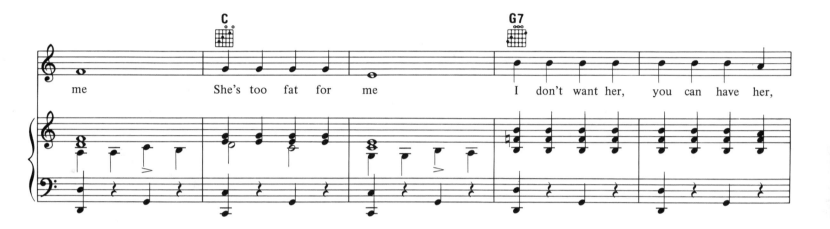

me She's too fat for me I don't want her, you can have her,

please do that for me She's too fat, she's too fat She's too fat for

me I get diz - zy,_____ I get num - bo_____ When I'm
She's a two - some,_____ She's a four - some_____ If she'd

Trio

Can she prance up a hill?_____ No! No! No! No!

No!_____ Can she dance a qua-drille?_____ No! No!

No! No! No!_____ Does she fit____ in my *coupe?_____

____ By her-self____ she's a group_____ Could she pos-si-bly

Sit up-on____ my knee? No! No! No!_____ Oh!

*pronounced "coop"

D.S. al Fine 𝄋

To last 16 bars of Chorus -

WHERE DID ROBINSON CRUSOE GO WITH FRIDAY ON SATURDAY NIGHT?

Words by SAM M. LEWIS and JOE YOUNG
Music by GEO. W. MEYER

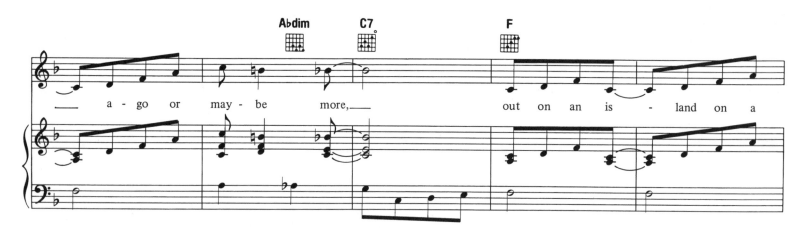

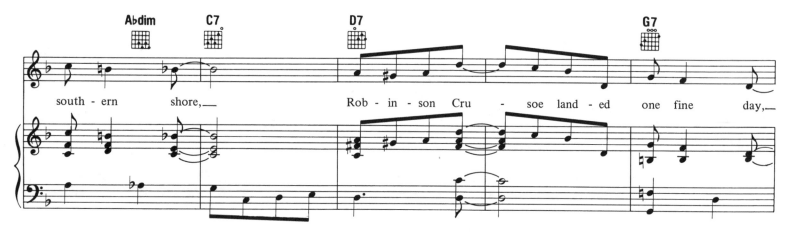

His good man Fri - day was his on - ly friend,___ they didn't bor -

row or lend; lend;_____ they built a lit - tle hut,

lived there 'til Fri - day, but Sat - ur - day night___ it was shut._____ And

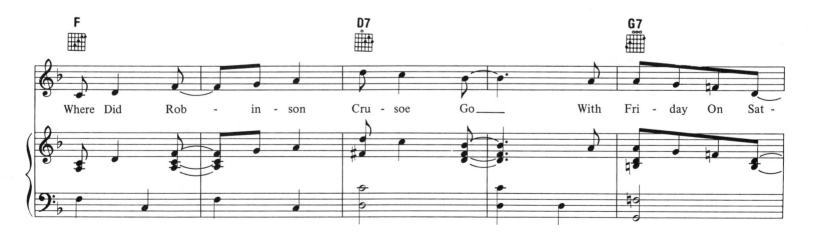

Where Did Rob - in - son Cru - soe Go___ With Fri - day On Sat -

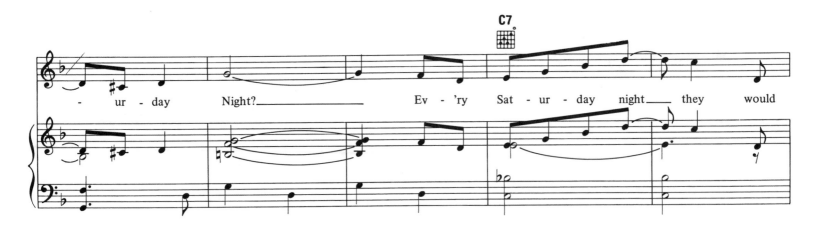

must be wild wo - men, so Where Did Rob - in - son Cru - soe Go

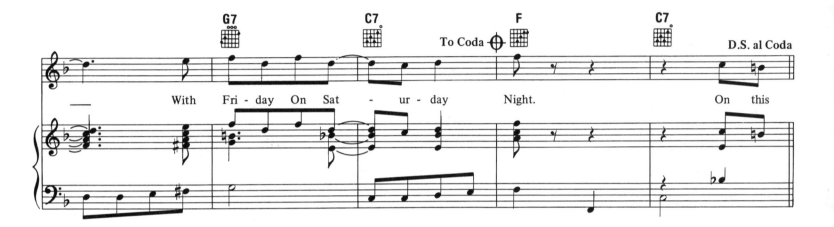

_ With Fri - day On Sat - ur - day Night. On this

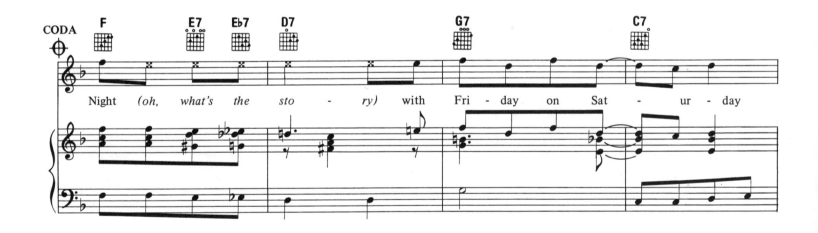

Night (oh, what's the sto - ry) with Fri - day on Sat - ur - day

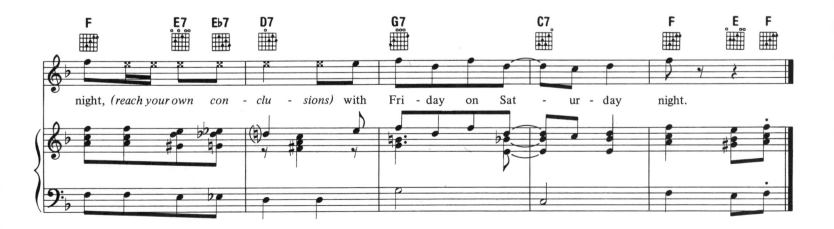

night, (reach your own con - clu - sions) with Fri - day on Sat - ur - day night.

WOOLY BULLY

Moderately

Words and Music by
DOMINGO SAMUDIO

1. Mat-ty told Hat-ty _____ a-bout a thing she saw.

Had two big horns _____ and a

wool-y jaw _____ Wool-y Bul-ly _____

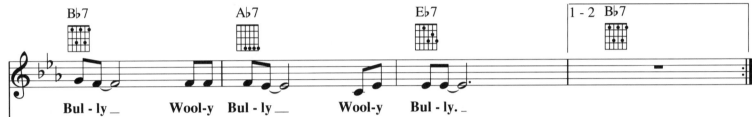

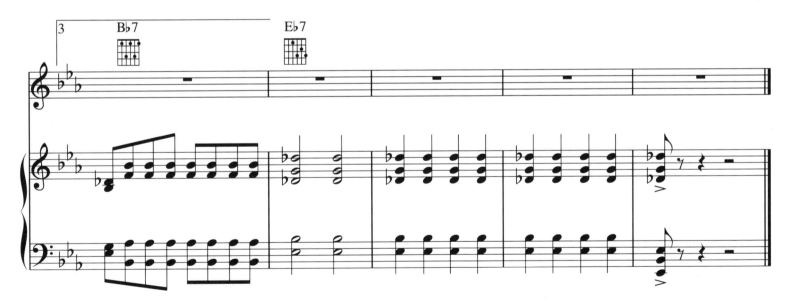

2. **Hatty told Matty**
   Let's don't take no chance,
   Let's not be L 7
   Come and learn to dance
   Wooly bully - wooly bully
   Wooly bully - wooly bully - wooly bully.

3. **Matty told Hatty**
   That's the thing to do,
   Get yo' someone really
   To pull the wool with you-
   Wooly bully - wooly bully
   Wooly bully - wooly bully - wooly bully.

YAKETY YAK

Words and Music by JERRY LEIBER
and MIKE STOLLER

YES! WE HAVE NO BANANAS

By FRANK SILVER and IRVING COHN

Moderately

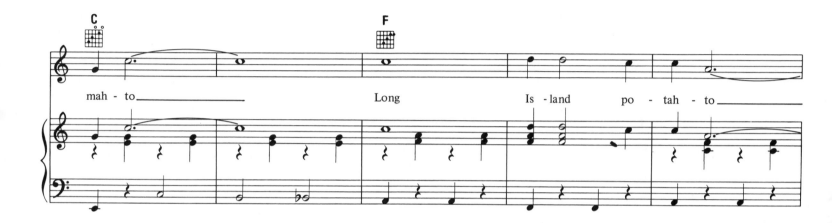

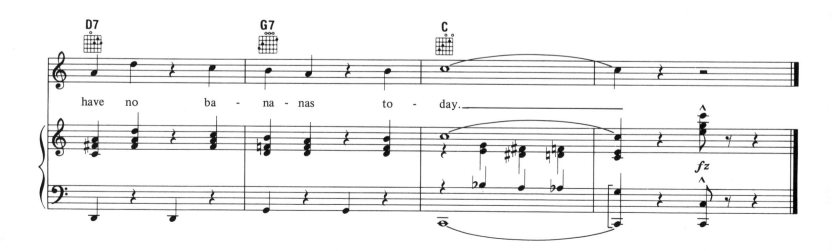

VAN LINGLE MUNGO

Arranged for Piano by DAVID FRISHBERG

Words and Music by
DAVID FRISHBERG